✧ ✧ ✧

Moments of Freedom

✧ ✧ ✧

Page-Barbour Lectures for 1996

✧ ✧ ✧

Moments of Freedom: Anthropology and Popular Culture

✧ ✧ ✧

Johannes Fabian

University Press of Virginia
Charlottesville and London

Publication of this book was assisted by a grant from
the Page-Barbour Lecture Fund

The University Press of Virginia

Printed in the United States of America

First published 1998

∞ The paper used in this publication meets the minimum requirements
of the American National Standard for Information Sciences—
Permanence of Paper for Printed Library Materials, ANSI Z39.48-1984.

Library of Congress Cataloging-in-Publication Data

Fabian, Johannes.
Moments of freedom : anthropology and popular culture / Johannes
Fabian.
p. cm.
"Page-Barbour lectures."
Includes bibliographical references and index.
ISBN 0-8139-1785-9 (cloth : alk. paper) — ISBN 0-8139-1786-7
(pbk. : alk. paper)
1. Ethnology—Congo (Democratic Republic)—Katanga. 2. Popular
culture—Congo (Democratic Republic)—Katanga. 3. Katanga (Congo)—
Social life and customs. I. Title.
GN654.F35 1998
306′.096751′8—dc21 97-42296
CIP

Contents

Illustrations

Preface and Acknowledgments

This book is based on field research I began more than thirty years ago in a region, Katanga, of a country then known as the Democratic Republic of the Congo. Mobutu Sese Seko (then still Joseph-Désiré by his Christian name) had just risen to power. A few years later he introduced certain symbolic measures to mark the country's break with its colonial past. Among them was a change of geographical and political names. Katanga became Shaba, R.D. Congo, as well as the river Congo, was to be called Zaire. Members of the opposition in exile never accepted this, and when the time came to break again, now with a postcolonial regime, names that the country had taken when it became independent were restored by the new president, Laurent Kabila. But a generation had grown up, or grown old, speaking and thinking of their country as Zaire. I doubt they will easily revert to names that are too close to colonial times. Zaire has a sound, a flavor; it stirs memories, good and bad. Zaire symbolizes the period I cover in these essays, but also its topics, the creations of popular culture, above all Zairian music. When the new names surprised us after the manuscript had gone into production, I decided to leave it as it was. I gained whatever insights I have during an era that has come to an end. This is what I want to express when I use Zaire and Zairian rather than Congo and Congolese.

Popular culture is a theme I am unable to address from the safe distance of some theoretical place above or some historical moment beyond. For thirty years I have been thinking, inquiring, and writing about representations and practices, beliefs and objects that make up popular culture in an urban African setting: labor and language, religious movements, theater and storytelling, music and painting, grassroots literacy and historiography.

Still being in the midst of these projects, I find it impossible to start with a disquisition on the concept of popular culture, let alone a definition of it. Instead, I shall begin in the middle, with a few reactions to what I perceive to be a climate that has become increasingly hostile toward the idea. Yes, popular culture is a problematic concept. But what concept worth exploring isn't? No, popular culture doesn't seem to get us away from problems we have with the concept of culture. What does? Class and gender, domination and power apparently don't. Yes, popular culture has become a fashionable concept; it often guides shallow, hit-and-run research. But the same goes for networks, modes of production, civilizing processes, regimes of power, and other ideas in vogue.

In the societies we come from, ordinary people eat and drink; they work and play, have families and watch television. Occasionally they do some culture, such as seeing a play or going to a concert. Anthropologists, who began by figuring out how human beings lived in faraway places or times, now think that more or less everything people do to get through life is CULTURE. (They also worry about what is *not* culture, usually by invoking nature—ecological and biological determinations—but this will not be my preoccupation in these essays.)

Serious thought about popular culture inevitably leads one to question the concept of culture itself. In fact the real subject of this book may be a kind of reckoning, an *Abrechnung* with CULTURE. Here is a short catalog of issues for debate that, at the same time, provides a sketch of the development of culture theory in anthropology as I see it.

There is first what might be called the classical modern concept. It affirms that culture is real, that it exists as a (complex) entity. This position of ontological realism held that culture existed as tradition outside individual minds. Tradition was envisaged as a collection of objects, symbols, techniques, and whatnot that could be shared by people at a given time and transmitted over time from one generation to another. This concept was formulated against earlier notions that held that culture was less a possession than a quality of persons or of collectivities (peoples, nations) and that it was something that could increase, decrease, and even get lost.

Being essentially a combination of traits, culture was thought to exist in the plural. In studies of culture the focus was on different, indeed unique, inventions and forms. This classical modern concept gave way to the modern concept as it was elaborated in structuralist-functionalist theory. Although it could encompass classical concerns (with the description, analysis, or interpretation of culture reified), it entailed a switch from what has been called intellectualism (Tylor) to moralism (Durkheim). The result was a sociologizing of culture. Its theoreticians wanted to explain, account for, and ideally, predict or manipulate "behavior." In its extreme forms this approach gave rise to purely statistical or purely structural theories of human conduct, even though many schools of modern anthropology tried to reconcile the opposites. One effect of such social-scientific fervor, not much noticed at the time, was that the question of culture's reality was quietly disposed of (or relegated to other disciplines). In postmodern theory, most of what was once identified as culture now appeared as discourse (including epistemes, regimes of power, disciplines, texts, etc.). As I see it, this was less a break with modern culture theory than a radicalization of it (see Clifford and Marcus 1986).

At present, thought about culture seems to have branched in two directions: a deconstructive, nonontological, nonpersonal (Foucault would have said nonhuman) conception and another that is centered on a constructive notion of culture as praxis.

The plot thickens with the rise of "global" theory (with its connections to world-system theory), which consciously attempts to save or recuperate the classical modern concept of reified culture by emphasizing commodification, circulation, and differential distribution of chunks of culture, all but abandoning the idea of culture as a boundary-maintaining, integrated system (to use some of the favorite vocables of modern theory).

I would situate my own struggles with culture, in which I here engage by a detour through popular culture, as follows: I share the opposition to a systemic integration view and see the alternative in a praxis approach that is compatible with what one might call neo-objectivism, inspired by Hegel and Marx and exemplified by recent material culture theory. It is also close to theories of embodiment (including the rehabilitation of the senses) with connections to feminist thought.

Since I want to keep my arguments close to ethnography, a brief description of the context is called for. The material to be presented comes from the towns of Shaba, the copperbelt in southeastern Zaire, bordering on Zambia. Copper mining on an industrial scale began in the first decade of this century; by the mid-twenties a large labor force had been "stabilized" by a policy of hiring married workers and settling them in company towns. Substantial towns grew up around the mines, including secondary industries, transportation, trade, education, and administration. A distinctive variety of Swahili emerged as an expression, as well as a medium, of a lively urban culture. Music and dance traditions from the workers' home regions were cultivated and transformed in ostensibly "tribal" mutual aid societies; religious movements created a new discourse and new rituals; mission schools, sports clubs, and youth organizations (such as the Boy Scouts) organized leisure activities; bars and dance halls favored modern music styles, performed on Western instruments, and became the stage for vaudeville-like entertainment including theatrical sketches; educational associations were formed, often with political goals; visual arts for local consumption by settled workers and an emerging petite bourgeoisie were the last to appear in this process. By the time the former Belgian Congo became an independent country in 1960, all these practices and expressions existed even though they remained unnamed and largely ignored by expatriate residents and most social scientists. The latter were preoccupied with the theoretical agendas of the fifties and sixties—urbanization and social change—questions whose urgency seemed to increase when the checks and controls that colonial regimes had put on African initiatives and mobility were removed. The suggestion that a concept such as popular culture might be required to understand contemporary African life would have convinced few before the mid-seventies.

In presenting my thoughts about popular culture I draw on my inquiries in Shaba. This approach means, on the one hand, that certain topics and domains repeatedly will be taken up, albeit in different contexts and for different purposes. On the other hand, the need to be selective and the limitations of my own firsthand experience can only result in an incomplete picture of contemporary life in that region. Aside from expressions of popular culture I know of but left untouched (I will name them in the conclusion), there must be others I never noticed, or could not have noticed because they have emerged since the mid-eighties, the last time I visited Shaba.

These essays have been an occasion not only to revisit earlier research projects but also to consider, and perhaps reconsider, some of the theoretical statements I have made over the years in articles and books about a religious movement (Fabian 1970), about Shaba popular painting (Szombati-Fabian and Fabian 1976; Fabian and Szombati-Fabian 1980), about popular painting, song, and religion (Fabian 1978), about the history of Shaba Swahili (Fabian 1986), about popular literacy and historiography (Fabian 1990a, 1996), and about proverbs and popular theater (Fabian 1990b).

A remark is in order regarding the autobiographic style in which I present not only research contexts and experiences, but also theoretical developments. Many find the use of the first person singular in scientific prose distasteful or irksome. I could point out that conventions have been changing and that I find myself in quite respectable company (see Geertz 1995; Goody 1995; Vansina 1994). In fact there are indications that first-person accounts that are not autobiographies in the usual sense are emerging as a genre of anthropological writing. A tempting explanation—in my view neither charitable nor correct—may be to put this down to the age of authors whose horizon is narrowing as they approach the end of their careers. Nor should autobiographic ethnography be mistaken for a symptom of rampant subjectivism. On the contrary, a serious argument can be made (though this is not the place to make it) that the autobiographic turn is connected with anthropology's turn to history. As the natural scientific paradigm with its built-in objectivity loses its hold on our discipline, we seek in history new ground for situating our objects of study as well as our ways of studying them. What else connects us to history other than our being part of it? How much the autobiographic in ethnography needs to be foregrounded is and will remain a matter of taste and debate; that ethnography is grounded in autobiography is not.

The chapters that follow developed from shorter texts originally written for oral presentation. Though they are connected by the theme of popular culture, each of them makes a new start, takes a different angle. The perspective from which I approach my topics is that of cultural anthropology, but I am not addressing only the expert. Especially in the first chapter, I have tried, through notes and bibliographical references, to locate my work in a wider context of research on popular culture in Africa and in other parts of the world. Power (chapter 2), time (chapter 3), and thought (chapter 4) are themes that have had my attention at different times. Writing this book has made me discover links between them that I was not aware of.

In earlier publications I expressed my gratitude to the many individuals and institutions who helped me with, or sponsored, research in Shaba. An inordinately long list would be required to name them all here and to do the same for the many people who were willing to listen to earlier versions and parts of the chapters of this book.

For providing the occasion to undertake this reflexive project I am indebted, above all, to the University of Virginia and members of the committee that invited me to deliver the 1996 Page-Barbour lectures. Allan Megill, Susan McKinnon, and my old friend Roy Wagner all had their part in convincing their colleagues that I would have something to say before they, or I, knew what it would be. As with horses, being bet on makes us run.

Finally, I want to thank Alice Bennett, who, resolutely yet tactfully, did the copyediting—not an easy task when the writer has a hybrid linguistic background.

✧ ✧ ✧

Moments of Freedom

✧ ✧ ✧

1

✧ ✧ ✧

Popular Culture in Anthropology

Culture versus Popular Culture

Some time ago Zygmunt Bauman, one of sharpest critics of the anthropological concept of culture, formulated an insight that can be the starting point for thought about popular culture. In his book *Culture as Praxis* he argued that there is little use trying to settle the question of what culture means; certainly it is useless to search for an unassailable definition. All talk about culture is talk, rhetoric, an argument designed to convince, a discourse claiming to present a certain kind of knowledge. As he put it, "The concept of culture, whatever its specific elaborations, belongs with the family of terms standing for human praxis" (Bauman 1973, 117). I read this to mean that what culture stands for, as well as our ways of making it stand for something, is human praxis. Though it makes sense to distinguish theory from practice, that distinction itself is made as part of a praxis of, say, scientific inquiry. Anthropological (or for that matter any kind of) culture theory is a kind of praxis.

Much like culture without a qualifier, popular culture signals discursive strategies and research practices that produce a certain kind of knowledge. When we add the qualifier "popular" to culture, we do so because we believe it allows us to conceptualize certain kinds of human praxis that the concept of culture without the qualifier either ignores or makes disappear. Although the two concepts do not differ in that they constitute practices, culture *tout court* is usually talked about as if it existed as an entity, as if it was there to be studied; discourse on popular culture tends to be about movements or processes rather than entities. Moreover, talk about popular culture in anthropology (but also in other fields, especially in history) has been argumentative, sometimes militant. As a negation or antonym of culture, popular culture contests integrative and normative conceptions (catchwords: system, beliefs, and values) that came to characterize modern structural-functional theories of culture that all but obliterated concern with freedom and power. As an affirmation, popular culture theory asserts the existence of spaces of freedom and creativity in situations of oppression and supposedly passive mass consumption.

In sum, determining what popular culture means is not a matter of semantics.[1] Pragmatics and rhetoric, in fact attention to political praxis, are required if we want to appreciate why and how the concept is being deployed in current research and writing (more on this in the last section of this chapter). Emphasis on the practical also implies that uses of popular culture are seen as embedded in historical conditions and that concept and term may take on different meanings depending on such contexts. It makes a difference whether popular culture in Europe and North America is opposed in predominantly aesthetic terms to high or elite culture; whether it becomes the political battle cry of "conscientization" and liberation in Latin America; whether it is defined by decree as the correct culture as happened, at least during a certain period, in "Popular" China; or whether it is being used, almost exclusively by academic intellectuals, in an effort to further our understanding of contemporary African culture by progressing from fixations on tribal traditions perishing under the onslaught of Westernization to appreciating the vital, often exuberant expressions modern Africans give to their experiences. It is only a slight exaggeration to state that contemporary African music, theater, painting, and sculpture, but also much of religion and politics, would not have become objects of research in anthropology had it not been for popular culture or some such notion. Of course those who live the contemporary African life may have no need for the concept of popular culture. "What you are talking about is our culture," an African participant recently told the audience at a symposium on popular culture in Africa.[2]

Before moving on, let us take conceptual stock. (Popular) culture is not an entity; the term stands for certain discursive strategies. Popular culture signals a discourse that raises issues of power, if only because it tends to contest what is being affirmed about culture. Although the approach sketched here denies ontological status to culture, this does not mean that culture and popular culture are merely analytical categories or heuristic devices. They are real enough as practices of inquiry and writing, addressed to real practices of living and embroiled in political relations and interests. This is why concepts such as (popular) culture are anything but a matter of definition. Consequently, when we want to defend the notion of popular culture, we should concentrate on what it makes appear and become known, rather than agonize about the adjective "popular."

From Culture to Popular Culture

But I am getting ahead of my story. Popular culture is by now accepted in anthropology as a distinctive concept and field of inquiry. It is for future historians of the discipline to show us how this happened. In the meantime, those of us who took the road from culture to popular culture can tell our stories.

In the sixties, when I prepared myself at an American university for dissertation research in Africa, the concept of culture was more in vogue than ever. It was the centerpiece of a "unified theory of action" (as the project was called) designed to bring together "behavioral sciences" such as anthropology, sociology, psychology, and political science.[3] Thought about culture, as it was propagated then, was said to have liberated itself from premodern connotations of a singular, hierarchical, elitist *Bildung* or *la civilisation*. Culture was universal, yet plural. That *was* progress, and we were conscious of it.

What did not bother us much was that culture had all but lost its militant connotations. Historically, contestation started with a defiant use of culture in the plural, challenging singular, exclusive, or hierarchical notions developed when, from Enlightenment and romantic beginnings, evolutionism emerged as one of the first paradigms of the discipline. Defiance was also the spirit that reigned when Franz Boas and his disciples set out to formulate a theory of culture designed to compete with racist doctrines in explaining how human behavior was determined.[4]

But culture, though conceived in a defiant, militant spirit, came out positive; it was made up of values and beliefs that oriented, directed, and organized action in systems it provided with their own logic. Culture gave purpose to the social system and ensured its equilibrium. Behavior that did not fit this ideal was abnormal, deviant, dysfunctional, and therefore—though I don't remember anyone's actually saying this—acultural or anticultural. Such was the enthusiasm for a structuralist-functionalist theory of culture that few suspected it of being a law-and-order concept that was not all that different from what our Enlightenment predecessors had in mind when they spoke of civilized societies as *sociétés policées*.

Equipped with such a powerful theory of culture, I set out to study the Jamaa, a religious movement in the Shaba region of Zaire. Like others of my generation, I approached my task critically. I was prepared to understand as creative and innovative a phenomenon that had previously been perceived and described as, at worst, curious, disturbing, misguided, and mixed up and as at best a "syncretist" result of acculturation and social change. Convinced that ideas rather than dire needs or uncontrolled drives were at the center of the Jamaa movement I had selected for study, I concentrated on doctrine and its transmission through teaching and initiation. Language became central in my investigations: the language in which the ideas were expressed, the distinctive vocabulary and rhetoric that characterized the doctrine, and the practices of speaking and communication that gave me access to it all. One of the attractions of such an approach was that, in a late colonial, early postcolonial context, it made anthropological research possible in a thoroughly modern urban-industrial world. I could do without a society, a tribe, or even a village; I had a movement.

I am not about to argue that all this reasoning—inspired as it was by a Weberian-Parsonian concept of culture—was misguided and misleading. In fact I am still rather proud of the work I did with the Jamaa, and I know that I laid then the foundation for what I have been doing since. It took many years and other projects in the same area before I realized that the productivity and elegance of the culture theory I started out with had a price. To express this in an image that is not all that exaggerated, the light this approach concentrated on the religious movement that was the object of study left in the dark the rest of the world of which it was a part. I knew how to converse about intricacies of doctrine but was utterly incapable of discussing the latest soccer match. I spent countless hours in the homes of followers (mostly mine workers with their families) where we gathered to listen to Jamaa teaching, but I paid little attention to the furniture, the pictures on the walls, or the clothes people were wearing. Day or night, in some corner of the miners' company town where I lived, people were playing records of Zairian music or drumming and dancing at a wake, wedding, or puberty rite. For me all this was little more than background noise, in contrast to the sounds of Jamaa *mafundisho* and hymns. What I took away from field research in the mid-sixties was the ethnography of a movement, presented as something not quite unique but highly distinctive and seemingly self-contained. I also knew the founder was the author of a book on Bantu philosophy that had an impact throughout Africa and beyond and that certain Jamaa tenets, such as the crucial rite of "encounter," were somehow part of an international (today we would say global) Christian lay movement inspired by social psychology. But all this was put aside, at least for the time being. I had yet to understand that the global is *in* the local.

Although it came slowly, I still experienced it as a revelation when, during another stay in Shaba from 1972 to 1974 and in the years that followed, I understood that the very language the Jamaa movement spoke, a variety of Swahili, was not just there, the way languages usually seem to be because we don't catch them at their birth. Shaba Swahili had been created not long before by people from many different corners of Zaire and neighboring countries who suddenly found themselves wage earners in towns. Much of the distinctive style of speaking and conversing I had discovered in the Jamaa turned out to be characteristic of public speech in the mining towns of Shaba. As a religious movement, the Jamaa was connected to similar grassroots appropriations and transformations of Christianity, and the members of the Jamaa shared with millions of other Zairians their petit bourgeois attitudes toward their living rooms, their ideas of a picture they would like to have on the wall or of a tune they would like to listen and dance to. In fact religion was just one domain and one kind of discourse that, together with music, painting, and theater, made up a vast complex of thought, representations, and performances. And that was popular culture.

I must note, however, that this discovery was anything but the predictable or actual result of the research project that had brought me back to Shaba. In my grant application and the extensive final report, I never invoked the concept of popular culture.[5] The theoretical frame I had formulated for this project was inspired by sociolinguistics and the ethnography of speaking. Its focus was on language and work in industrial and artisanal contexts. Documentation concentrated on lexical-semantic classification, on speech events and communicative exchanges, as well as on reflections and life histories, all of them recorded at work or in workers' homes. By that time I had moved away from the kind of systemic, symbol- and meaning-centered notion of culture described earlier. Still, even in its communication-centered and pragmatic form, what I called culture without a qualifier continued to guide my research. I thought of other pursuits, such as my contacts with popular theater and painting, as fascinating yet rather incidental extensions of my sociolinguistic project. Almost reluctantly, I began to use the term "workers' culture" to express the growing insight that all of this, from the semantics of technical terms in Swahili to the intriguing paintings of mermaids I noticed on the walls of workers' living rooms, was somehow connected. "Urban culture" would have been an alternative designation; urban anthropology was by then an established subdiscipline. For several reasons, only some of which I can put into words, I never thought my work should be classified as urban anthropology. True, large modern towns were the sites where I conducted field research; their emergence and functioning, and especially their alleged effect of uprooting peasants who moved into them, however, were not problems I started out with. All I saw were people who tried to make a living and enjoyed life if and when they had the modest means to do so. Unlike some of the best urban anthropology of the time, my entry to this urban culture had been neither youth oriented nor poverty oriented. The members of the Jamaa were adult married couples; most of the men were among the best-paid wage earners in the country. At any rate, much work in urban anthropology was, for my taste, too sociological, interested in relations, networks, and classes in which urbanites were caught up, not in what people living in towns created.

In the introduction to a collection of his essays, *Scenes from African Urban Life* (1992), A. L. Epstein, a member of the Manchester (that is, the dissident, rather leftish) school of British anthropology, gives us a glimpse of how confining one of the reigning paradigms in anthropology was when it came to studying African life in towns. Epstein conducted research on the Zambian copperbelt in the 1950s, covering, as he says, mainly "the conventional rubrics." Eventually he became aware of the "distinctive flavor" of African life and permitted himself to be distracted from his serious work on social change by such divertissements as the inventive, often playful and funny ways urban people had with the Bemba language when they created a new variety that was spoken in the towns. Studying social networks was fine, but "there was a more direct route, to some extent *opened up by the greater freedom I enjoyed in Ndola for personal contact with Africans* but also by the rich material gathered by my research assistants, whose reports were studded by vernacular expressions employed by their collocutors. I am referring, of course, to language" (1992, xv; my emphasis).

Today his "Linguistic Innovation and Culture on the Copperbelt" (1959) is a classic. But when Epstein showed the paper to Max Gluckman, the leader of the Manchester school, Gluckman suggested that he submit this stuff on language and culture to an American journal (presumably because language and culture were not subjects to be taken seriously by social anthropologists at the time). Epstein goes on to note that

> Gluckman [also] expressed doubts of quite another kind about the paper, feeling that my material was presented in such a way as to hold the African up to ridicule. I appreciated Gluckman's sensitivity in the matter, but it also seemed to me that, in so far as some of the matter might provoke laughter, he failed to see that there is an important difference between laughing at and laughing with people. . . . Seen from this point of view, the new language of the towns was a creative response; with its wit and inventiveness *CiCopperbelti* served Africans as a means of placing their own distinctive stamp on this otherwise alien and often oppressive milieu. (1992, xv–xvi)

Gluckman was guided by an ethos of scientific seriousness that he shared with Malinowski and Radcliffe-Brown. I doubt he would have taken kindly to the observation that his position expressed a kind of puritan disdain. Social theory, being concerned with order and identity, was at a loss when it came to dealing with the anarchic disrespect for rules and the self-mockery that were cultivated by urban Africans, not only in their ways with language.

Epstein felt no need to introduce the concept of popular culture, and he could not have come "from culture to popular culture" because for him, as a British social anthropologist, culture was not a point of departure (in the index of his book neither "culture" nor "popular culture" rates an entry). Still, I quoted him at length because he more than anticipated an insight that came to me during research on the Jamaa movement and, developed further, eventually led me to the "discovery" of popular culture as a guiding concept: Language and communication play a crucial role not only in our research, but also in providing practical foundations for life in the towns. As far as traditional societies were concerned, the "tribal" language was assumed to provide identity even by those who thought of talking as rather epiphenomenal to acting. Vehicular languages in the towns, like "syncretist" religious movements and various theatrical enactments known as "dances," were regarded as disconnected symptoms of the loss of tribal identity.[6] Epstein had also hit, at least implicitly, on an idea that was to be taken up and developed twenty years later, namely that the linguistic processes that produced languages like CiCopperbelti—pidginization and creolization—may offer models for understanding other expressions of popular culture.[7]

To return to my own story, by the mid-seventies I decided to set aside work on the Jamaa and to postpone narrowly linguistic or sociolinguistic analysis of materials collected for the language and work project. Both projects had been theory driven; they were carefully reasoned out and planned beforehand, something that I began to realize could well have resulted in my finding out what I already knew had I not been forced by circumstances to radicalize my initial turn to language. That culture was like language was a long-held conviction, certainly among American and French anthropologists; that living a culture was like speaking was not such a popular idea (interest was in symbols and semiotics, meanings and codes, more than in pragmatics); and the notion that investigating a culture was a matter of productive communication was even less so. Without my being conscious of the connection at the time, increasing involvement with popular African culture made me feel more keenly just how ill equipped anthropological discourse was to deal with contemporaneity.[8] By mid-1973 I concluded the project on language and labor but stayed on in Shaba, taking a full-time position at the university. This change of roles changed the ways I experienced life in the city "after work." Getting to know Lubumbashi was now a matter of field leisure rather than fieldwork: I began taking in what came my way, enjoying purposeless conviviality, following my curiosity more than a research plan. My relations to the Jamaa relaxed, and I spent time hanging out—the best way to describe my contacts—with a group of local actors (most of them also accomplished musicians and dancers). I took a keen interest in the numerous paintings I discovered on the walls of living rooms, drinking places, and small shops. It did not take long before I began to pursue these new interests more systematically, recording conversations and performances and collecting a representative sample of pictures. Also, the more fluent I became in local Swahili, the more I realized that this language was not just a medium or vehicle but a way of life whose linguistic medium or expression told its own history and present predicament, effortlessly combining classical Bantu elements with innovations and borrowing from French and local languages.

As far as I can reconstruct things now, when I left Zaire at the end of 1974 to take a job at an American university, I was ready to recast my various researches as so many approaches to popular culture. I continued to explore theoretical issues raised by the turn to language (notably with work on the concept of genre that will have our attention in the next chapter) and published first results of research on popular painting.[9] In 1977 I applied unsuccessfully to the agency that had sponsored research on language and labor for funds to work on a synthesis of previous work. The project was titled "Work, Art, and Communication: Urban Culture in a New Nation." Instead of the projected book, I wrote a tentative and programmatic essay, "Popular Culture in Africa: Findings and Conjectures" (1978), that, although anything but conclusive, did conclude my journey from culture to popular culture and seems to have contributed to putting the issue on the agenda of African studies.

Popular Culture and History

Disciplinary constraints reflecting fascination with stable culture (in American cultural anthropology) or with stable social structure (in British social anthropology) were one reason popular culture went more or less unnoticed. Another reason, strange as it may sound, was the thoroughly ahistorical approach to social change taken by social and cultural anthropology. History seemed irrelevant as far as traditional societies were concerned; almost by definition, they were supposed to have remained the same at least as long as their existence had been documented. "Peoples without history" was a synonym for "primitives" and other designations for societies supposedly untouched by history. Like so many other pronouncements that came easily to anthropological discourse, the denial of history was by no means straightforward. On one hand, history was equated with development and change: with "natural history" under the evolutionist paradigm, with "universal history" under diffusionism. On the other hand, history "proper" was reserved to the West that made it. History was acknowledged to happen among Europe's others only to the extent that they suffered it. Throughout most of this century, the "uprooted masses" in urban Africa were depicted as the ones who suffered most from "Westernization." Such concern was dictated both by ethics and by ideological preconceptions that made it all but impossible to consider what happened in African towns as history. Apparent lack of historical depth and actual lack of historical knowledge led students of African urban life to adopt theoretical constructs that allowed them to conceive of social change (or adaptation) as a dynamic, but ahistorical because "systemic," response to outside "factors" such as industrialization and Western education.[10]

Paradoxically, the 1950s and 1960s, when ahistorical studies of contemporary social and cultural elements prevailed in anthropology (encouraged by structuralism, functionalism, and structuralism-functionalism), were also the moment when the theoretical and, above all, methodological tools for the study of African history, based on oral traditions, were forged and set to work.[11] Most of the energy in this soon flourishing field, however, was directed to traditional political entities. Histories of African cities were rare. A notable exception that helped direct my attention toward developments I was later to call popular culture was a history of Elisabethville (now Lubumbashi) by Bruce Fetter (1976). As much as it was possible, given the biases and constraints of the time (the mid-1960s) when he conducted his research, Fetter relied on African witnesses to the town's history (Elisabethville had been incorporated in 1911; mining operations leading to initial agglomerations started in 1906). He also found a wealth of information on collective efforts that the supposedly passive victims of urbanization undertook to preserve what they wanted to save of their heritage and to create new forms of sociality (Fetter 1974). In Elisabethville, as elsewhere in Africa, these efforts were known as "ethnic associations," a term eagerly taken up by urban sociologists and anthropologists because it served to cover a conceptual gap and lack of information about African life between tradition and modernity. In retrospect, one feels that the notion of associations (often called "voluntary" to mark their spontaneous origin and to distinguish them, presumably, from necessary or imposed institutions) also had its use in fending off suspicions that Africans might be engaged in political mobilization. In the Congo, political parties were not allowed until the very end of colonial rule in 1960, though ethnic associations (and religious movements such as the Kitawala) were probably always suspected of using their cultural, folkloric activities as a cover for resistance and subversion.

One of the documents Fetter collected (without making much use of it in his book) was the remarkable *Vocabulary of the Town of Elisabethville*. It was commissioned by an "association" of former domestic servants and written or compiled by an African resident of the town, André Yav (see Fabian 1990a). This history, written in one of the local varieties of Swahili, covered colonization, urbanization, industry, and communication, but it also addressed daily life, entertainment, and urban lore. It happens to be the only document of its kind and scope we have for the region at this moment. There are reasons to assume that other histories were written and circulated and that this evidence for grassroots literacy (meaning texts that were produced spontaneously, without prompting from expatriate persons or institutions, in a language that most people were never taught to write) was not of recent origin.[12]

In a newspaper published in Elisabethville before World War I a reporter informed his (presumably mostly expatriate) readers of a curious encounter with a recent African immigrant who spent his free time collecting and writing down the "customs" of the people. The journalist let it be known that, for a fee, he was allowed to glance at these writings. This prompted a stern reply (in French) in the same paper by the African concerned, confirming his work but categorically denying that money had passed between him and the reporter. As far as we can tell, this was the first documentation of "urban ethnography" in the colony. It also remained the only time an African was given a voice in the local press until the 1930s.[13]

These examples of recordkeeping, chronicling, and indeed historiography, written by Africans for Africans, no matter how incidental and unsystematic they may have been, show that urban Africans have been affirming what sociologists often denied and largely ignored: that concerning life in the city there is a story to be told, protagonists to be introduced, and a plot to be unraveled—a story other than the artificial, jerky moves of "change" and "adaptation" granted to Africans in the scientific literature until not long ago.

My own work took me to history on two roads, one direct, the other somewhat circuitous. The former was opened up by the discovery of popular painting in Shaba that turned out to be an "art of memory" providing images for the recollections of life in towns by people living there. At the time, about a decade after Zairian independence, these experiences tended to coincide with those of colonial rule. After some early reports on that discovery (see above), it took another decade and a half before I got around to my most recent project. This undertaking is a presentation and ethnography of what must count as one of the most remarkable works of popular historiography anywhere: a history of Zaire as painted and told by the Shaba genre painter Tshibumba Kanda Matulu (Fabian 1996).

I came to this formidable task prepared by an edition of the *Vocabulary of the Town of Elisabethville* mentioned above (Fabian 1990a), a text whose importance as direct evidence for popular historiography I had realized ever since Bruce Fetter gave me a copy in 1966. Like others who had copies of the document, I did nothing with it for more than twenty years, not only because other projects left me little time but also because the *Vocabulary*'s linguistic form made it forbiddingly difficult until I felt up to the task, having meanwhile taken what I referred to as my indirect road to history and the popular culture of Shaba. About 1978 I had begun to collect references to and copies of early descriptions of Swahili as spoken in the Congo, especially in the mining region of Katanga-Shaba (word lists, language manuals for colonial agents and missionaries, rudimentary grammars and phrase books). For a while I thought of my search (preferably for obscure and bad writings) as a hobby. But when I found the time to place this genre and corpus in its political and social context, matters became seriously interesting. The result was *Language and Colonial Power,* a colonial and social history of the emergence and appropriation of Swahili under Belgian rule (Fabian 1986).

To explain the importance of this study for my understanding of popular culture I need to go back, briefly, to doubts concerning African urban sociology and anthropology I began to have soon after my early work on the Jamaa. I suspected that certain theoretical orientations (not to speak of ideological interests) caused us to ignore cultural creations that had emerged in the cities. Eventually I realized that such blindness was a matter of commission, not just omission. When I undertook to write *Language and Colonial Power* I was guided by the idea that, because we had buried it ourselves, we should be able uncover the evidence that might radically change our views of the history of popular Swahili—an argument, I believe, that can be extended to much of African popular culture. Colonial writing on Swahili had been of two kinds. One was resolutely practical and purported to represent the language as actually spoken, mainly in the context of industrial work and in exchanges between foreign residents and their African domestic servants, day laborers, and helpers in commerce. Not surprisingly, what these manuals described was a reduced, pidginized variety that failed to represent the language urban Africans spoke among themselves. The other genre, sponsored mainly by the missions, was guided by the aim to codify and standardize a high-level variety that would be appropriate for literary and religious use (similar to east coast Swahili, which was being standardized at about the same time by British colonial authorities). Again the result was a largely imaginary language spoken by no one, including those who had been taught to employ it in writing and in formal contexts such as religious teaching.

Here, I concluded, was a historically well documented instance of quite different, but complementary, colonial control interests that had created spaces of freedom in which Shaba Swahili, a language whose vitality shows no signs of weakening more than a generation after the end of direct colonial rule, could emerge and develop. Creolization was a handy concept to characterize this emergence of vehicular media between high and traditional culture, and I began to suggest that other forms, such as various popular arts, might be approached as outgrowths of creolization (Fabian 1978, 317). I never worked this out in detail, and today I realize this was all for the better. Any theory that sets out to demonstrate that linguistic models apply in other areas of culture works, to say the least, with analogies that in effect deny the historical specificity of cultural creation or, worse, the historical nature of culture itself. Homologies, resemblances due to common historical origins, are another matter. As distinctive practices, languages such as Shaba Swahili may make it possible for popular culture to keep together forms of expression such as music, dance, theater, painting, magic and religion, and historiography (or to switch freely from one to another), forms that are often kept apart by class and institutional boundaries in high culture. Many of the creators of popular culture I got to know in Shaba were "multimedia" artists; their audiences, as far as I could tell, were multimedia consumers. They had to be, because many of the messages contained in artistic creations and performances, especially those that were appreciated for their finesse and political courage, were assembled from different media and genres: songs citing proverbs, paintings evoking songs, religious movements cultivating drumming and dancing, political speeches assuming religious registers, historical accounts citing contemporary songs or traditional fables, and so forth. It is this closeness to origins that accounts for the particular historicity of popular culture, a trait that indeed has its homology in the type of language Swahili represents. Although they may appear deceptively simple in grammar and lexicon, creoles must be lived—practiced in context—to be spoken expertly. They make formidable demands on communicative competence as distinguished from linguistic competence. Translating texts, often even merely transcribing them from recordings, can be a daunting task. Similarly, to perceive and interpret the richness of popular expression requires historically situated, shared knowledge that an ethnographer can never fully acquire. The study of "humble" popular culture teaches us humility.[14]

One matter that arises in these remarks on popular culture and history needs to be clarified. The attentive reader may be troubled when I speak here and elsewhere of the creators of popular culture as "artists." Am I lumping or confusing art and culture? There are several ways to meet this question. First of all, producers of popular culture, such as popular musicians, painters, and actors, speak of themselves as artists. When they reflect on what they do they often identify their practices and creations as art and, in that respect, seem to set themselves apart from prophets, practitioners of magic, and historians. On the other hand, the historical juncture at which

I encountered popular culture in Zaire does not permit the conclusion that art is perceived as a separate, let alone higher, domain of culture. If there are indications of an aesthetic distinction of art from mundane pursuits, there are many more indications of economic, practical inclusion. In conversations I had with actors and painters, they usually stressed that what they did was work and that, in the words of the painter Tshibumba, "work is one." In other words, although some creators of popular culture, being aware of concepts that circulate globally, freely speak of art as their vocation, it would be historically questionable to project onto African popular culture an opposition between art and work (or more specifically between arts and crafts) that is of comparatively recent origin even in Western talk about culture.[15]

Popular Culture and Freedom

I quoted Epstein expressing awareness of a link between researchers' freedom and their ability to perceive certain aspects of African urban life. Today we realize that the very perception of a vast number of elements as instances or parts of popular culture was made possible only once ethnographers were liberated from constraints imposed by reigning theories, whether functionalism (sometimes with Marxist or socialist leanings) or structuralism-functionalism (few of whose adherents could be suspected of such leanings). For a long time anthropology was blind to popular culture in Africa, in the right eye as much as the left.[16] Critical self-awareness, as well as knowledge accumulated during the past generation or so, seems to have liberated us from strictures of anthropological theory that caused Gluckman to discourage work like Epstein's. The study of popular culture in Africa is alive and growing.[17]

But researchers' freedom is not the kind that first comes to mind when we talk about popular culture as resistance, as a means of liberation, as "weapons of the weak." No doubt we made progress in our understanding when we recognized African "adaptations" to urban-industrial conditions as creative and as assertive of the right to give shape and meaning to one's life. But there is still more to learn when we realize that popular culture emerging under colonial domination *demanded freedom* in more than one sense: politically, it *asked* for freedom for the people; theoretically, it *required* freedom among those who created and lived it. Oppression as such does not generate creative response;[18] that is why quasi-mechanical models of "culture contact" did little to help us understand what happened when contact took place. Not mere exposure to power and oppression, but transformation of experience into communicable expressions, is at the origin of popular culture as resistance to colonial and postcolonial domination.

That freedom must exist for cultural creation to take place is, I believe, a position that needs to be maintained even if actual conditions in most postcolonial African countries, certainly in Zaire, seem to make it difficult to credit popular culture with much liberation. On the other hand, the demise of the apartheid regime created a climate of optimism that has led to a veritable explosion of studies of popular culture and its role in the struggle for freedom in South Africa. The longer I think about it, the more I am convinced that work on popular culture helps us to revive and keep alive the problem of freedom as an issue in anthropological theory.

The theoretical foundations for modern anthropology were laid in Enlightenment and romantic thought or, perhaps more accurately, in a confrontation between the two movements. Freedom, the philosophes argued, was a condition for emancipated citizens to exercise their faculties of reason and moral choice; romantic thinkers, while accepting this as a matter of principle, celebrated freedom as the prerequisite of artistic creation and as the essence of historical process. Both movements faced a problem (and proposed various solutions): How could they maintain these convictions in the face of necessity (of natural law) and destiny (as embodied in tradition)? To make a very long story very short, the tragedy of anthropology has been that, in its desire to establish itself as a science (or because of being pressured by the powers that be), it came to approach its subject—hominization, humanization, emancipation—through theories that were fraught with ideas bestowed on it by Newtonian physics and positivist sociology. Anthropology may have started out by thinking of the "human career" in terms of freedom—freedom from animal fear and destructive instincts, from religious or political dictates, from racism and other forms of biological determinism. It may have found in the concept of culture a tool for such thought; yet it always seems to have wound up with determinist, integrationist theories of human action. The most powerful and influential conceptualizations of culture—such as Boas's classical "linguistic" model[19]—ended by stressing necessity rather than freedom in explaining how culture worked, irrespective of individual choice or consciousness, by the rules of a supraindividual logic. The eventual demise of extreme culturalism was brought about less by reinstating freedom as a condition of both creating and living culture than by acknowledging the ambiguities of "meaning." Even singular traditions permit plural interpretations. Culture may no longer be imagined as an authoritative charter but rather can be seen as an entertaining, albeit serious, game. But norms and rules are tenacious concepts and tend to resurface in different guises—as grammar or style, for instance, or as discourse and genre.

At any rate, whenever the occasion arises to consider relations between culture and freedom, it has been common in modern anthropology to align freedom with the individual and culture with the collective. But that cannot be the only way to relate these concepts to each other. Culture can be the source of individual freedom in situations of collective oppression, and the most significant achievement of popular culture may be to create collective freedom precisely in situations where individual freedom is denied or limited. But that immediately sets up a quandary: Does this mean, as has been suggested explicitly (by those in our tradition who cannot think of freedom except as the freedoms accorded to the bourgeois subject), that popular culture has its principal use in controlling the masses by creating a collective illusion of something that can exist only individually? And so on and so forth.

When we introduce freedom into the discussion of popular culture, it seems that questions keep multiplying and the issue gets more and more confused. This, I hear colleagues argue, is what you get when you leave the ground of problems posed by empirical research and engage in speculations that our Enlightenment and romantic predecessors were so fond of. Yet I am not ready to grant what such objections ask me to grant: that there can be a purely philosophical point of departure in addressing freedom; the issue is always political, hence historically situated. So we may have to make another start: there is no justification for using the concept of freedom quasi-logically, a priori, in distinguishing high from low, elite from popular culture. This works both ways: elite-high culture is not a priori more free than mass-popular culture; conversely, expressions of high culture are not in themselves oppressive, and creations of popular culture are not in themselves liberating. Both assume such qualities only as part of a concrete political praxis. The problem of freedom poses itself *within,* not only *between,* high and popular, dominant and dominated culture. Our understanding of the particular history of oppression in which anthropology played its parts of collaborator and critic will not improve as long as we continue to imagine freely acting colonizers facing passive subjects acting only under coercion, or freedom-loving people resisting regimes and their agents that were just puppets of capitalist-imperialist economics and ideology. (Though the latter is certainly the more interesting proposition, if only because it goes against the grain of imperialism studies.) To state this position is anything but a denial of the facts of domination and oppression. It is a way of radicalizing the question and may clear a way out of the frequently stultifying reifications that seem to be the price of our justified and long overdue critique of anthropology's implication in colonialism and imperialism.

If freedom is conceived not just as free will plus the absence of domination and constraint, but as the potential to transform one's thoughts, emotions, and experiences into creations that can be communicated and shared, and if "potential," unless it is just another abstract condition like absence of constraint, is recognized by its realizations, then it follows that there can never be freedom as a state of grace, permanent and continuous. As a quality of the process of human self-realization, freedom cannot be anything but contestatory and discontinuous or precarious. Freedom, in dialectical parlance, comes in moments. That is an idea I brought away from many years of work on popular culture; it inspired the title for this book. Hence the concrete instances I will examine should also be understood as moments that provided insight rather than as cases systematically collected.

We should expect such an approach to be criticized as utopian and politically objectionable. It seems that in the singular freedom, like culture, is a thoroughly undemocratic concept. Must freedom be thought of in the plural? That it can be talked about in the plural is a matter of record. There are (historical) usages—for instance, *Freiheiten,* limited privileges and dispensations granted by rulers and governments long before the ideal of general freedom and emancipation was conceived. Later, when freedom was enshrined as a supreme value in revolutionary constitutions, plurality quickly reemerged in a host of adjectival qualifications, codified and classified as kinds of freedom from or of *x, y, z.* When at one point I used the search words "freedom" and "culture" to browse through the online catalog of an American university library (not the best, not the worst), I made an interesting observation. I found only three works listed under freedom without a qualifier (one of them turned out to be a book on the concept of freedom in Lessing or Goethe). There were endless lists of items on what I called freedom with adjectival qualifications. By far the longest (length reflecting number of works in the library) was made up of entries treating "freedom of the press." However limited the value of such a survey may be, it says something about the place of freedom in public academic consciousness.

Of course further objections may be raised against this attempt to make freedom again an issue in our theorizing about culture. What counts, one could say, are freedoms, civil liberties, rights whose exercise must be unimpeded and whose violation should be prosecuted and punished. Such a quasi-legal understanding of freedom is, it seems, much better suited to empirical inquiries into relations between freedom and popular culture. Up to a point this is undoubtedly so, though it is not certain that such studies would come up with simple "more rights more popular culture" results. Restrictions of mobility, limited access to education, censoring of the press and other publications, controls on religious and other associations, imposed official languages and literacies, expropriation of land and forced cultivation, ethnic identities invented for administrative purposes—all of them were denials of basic rights practiced during colonial times. They must have stifled free and creative development of cultural expression, though we can only guess to what extent. We don't have to guess, we know, that in the former Belgian Congo deportation of religious leaders, for instance, spread new religious messages throughout the colony. Intellectual acumen or even genius that could not express itself in institutions of higher learning was applied to informal philosophies and histories that outlived official ideologies. Attempts, often benevolent, to promote what counted as African art hardly made a dent in the rise of popular painting, music, and dance. In fact, repressive institutions such as the colonial army became the cradle, or at least a cradle, of the Zairian popular music that was later to sweep the continent (Kazadi 1979). Political opinion and critique, prohibited by the regime, were channeled into ironic song texts and theatrical comedy. Institutions aimed at controlling the youth and the workforce, such the Boy Scouts and other youth associations, sports organizations, and the like, produced networks, practices, discourses, and channels for leadership the colonizers would never have dreamed of encouraging. Most of these hard-won spaces of freedom remained open when, after a brief period of euphoric hope, absentee colonialism maintained a totalitarian regime that caused many Africans to entertain nostalgic views of colonial times. Should all of this be dismissed as sentimentalism only because, in the approach I advocate here, I argue that it cannot be understood without introducing into our theory a historically romantic (not sentimental) notion of freedom as a condition of popular culture?

Alterity and Popular Culture

In my thought, research, and writing, anthropology and popular culture have been linked. There is of course no reason to assume that for other anthropologists, or other students of popular culture, this link is as natural and inevitable as I came to perceive it. What counts as an object of anthropological study is a matter of debate. A widespread opinion, reflected in current research practices, holds that anthropology, being a kind of natural science of conduct and culture, can and should direct its attention to "all things human," from cocktail waitressing to head-hunting (actually, the other way around, since an evolutionary perspective usually goes with the natural science view). I belong to those who believe that, although our discipline's future may be open, its past is not. Ours is a science that not only is de facto historically situated (all sciences are), but whose practice, from lofty theory down to methods and techniques, requires that we understand our place in history. How we assumed and maintained that place is open to informed interpretation (and in that sense the past is open, after all). But there can be no doubt that the emergence of anthropology is tied to the question of alterity. Anthropology did not find its object, it construed it as an other. If that is so, otherness is an issue in whatever anthropology undertakes to study, including popular culture.

Let me illustrate this point, again with a focus on Africa. In colonial times, many expressions we would now consider part of popular African culture (dress fashions, forms and places of entertainment, living styles, use of European languages, religious syncretism) were perceived (and represented) as inept apings, inauthentic copies of Western culture. Often they were called funny; most of the time they were quickly denounced as ridiculous. Why couldn't colonials just have fun with what they perceived as funny? Why did they become defensive-aggressive when they saw that Africans had taken hold of something the Europeans considered theirs?[20] The most plausible reason (remember Gluckman's embarrassment and anxiety when he was faced with Epstein's funny CiCopperbelti) seems to be that such features were experienced as threatening, or at any rate not fitting, constructions of the colonized as an other. Actually, colonial discourse construed two kinds of alterity (a distinction that was important to colonial ideology): the traditional, rural other as the true native, and the modern, urban other as the alienated native. The distinction served to keep the native *authentic* as an other for an authentic self. To get through to the true African, to discover genuine African thought, was an aim proclaimed by colonial administrations and missions from the early days on. The more authenticity was construed as part of the colonial scheme of things, the more urgent it became to find such authenticity locally, in tribal tradition. Modernity was to be brought to Africa, not achieved there; the trick of "native policies" was to control and if necessary to withhold modernity whenever actual modern Africans made their presence felt.

Theories of modernization shared a tragic stance that had been cultivated by anthropology since its beginnings: the peoples the West came in contact with were said to be doomed; ethnography's objects were always disappearing objects. In anthropology, theory of culture established itself as a theory of disappearance (Fabian 1991, chap. 10). Almost a century before the 1950s, the decade when studies of the purportedly disastrous effects of modernization were at their peak, lamenting the disappearance of tradition, travelers and ethnographers hit that note when they decried incipient urbanization (some of which predated the effective establishment of colonial rule). The destructiveness of ethnology was now seen to be at work once removed (or redoubled): the theoretically disappearing native, victim of imposed images, disappears practically in towns that are the sites of modernity. Leo Frobenius, the celebrated Africanist, waxed poetic (as he was wont to do) when he concluded his dirge *Das sterbende Africa: Die Seele eines Erdteils* (Dying Africa: The soul of a continent) with this appeal to students of Africa's past:

> Grabt!
> Aber achtet darauf, daß die Scherben nicht euch begraben.
> Erlebt!
> Unter jenen, die durch uns sterben.
> Sterben müssen.
> Erlebt es vor ihrem Tode.
> Damit ihr die Wiederaufstehung verstehen lernt!

> [Keep digging! But see to it that the sherds don't bury *you*. Experience life. Among those who die through us. Must die. Experience it before they die. So that you learn to understand resurrection.] (1928, 503)

Did he have a premonition of the emergence of a vigorous contemporary African culture? Or even of the practical and theoretical learning processes that were required to perceive modern African culture as something in its own right?

Before I go on to consider aspects of our discipline's history that may account for a special kind of affinity between anthropology and popular culture, I would like to take another crack at interpreting negative reactions to African modernity. Though this inevitably simplifies matters, it could be said that *imitation* was a key concept in colonial perceptions of popular culture (*evolution,* as in *évolué,* a particularly Belgian epithet for modern Africans, was always in the background, *assimilation* often in the foreground of colonial discourse). *Adaptation* was another term current especially in (Catholic) theories of missionizing and deserves more attention than I can give it here. It had its precedents as far back as the sixteenth-century debates between Jesuits and Franciscans about how far Chinese philosophy and customs could be integrated with Christianity. In its modern version, adaptation allowed for a two-way process whereby elements of traditional African culture—art, architecture, music, and dance—were envisaged as contributing to a contemporary, yet specifically African Christianity.

In postcolonial times *creativity* became a key concept in studies of social change. Remember this was *the* critical concept that inspired the study of African religious movements as it moved from cataloging African reactions to Christianity to conceptualizing innovative appropriations and new syntheses.[21] This change of paradigms—which marked my own trajectory—was at first directed against dominant, modern culturalism and its inability to conceive of process as anything but "change" (conceptualized around notions such as deviance, dysfunctional impact, and the reestablishment of social equilibrium). Is it correct to say that the "creative native" replaced the "disappearing native"? Tradition had, perversely, been thought of as disappearance (perversely, because talk of tradition seemed to emphasize the force of time and the weight of history while in fact it served to describe disappearance as removal from time and contemporaneity). This view established a new danger and a task for critical reflection: Is "creative popular culture" once again just a foil for construing an other against a perception of the Western self caught up in inauthentic mass production and consumption? I leave these questions unanswered for the time being. In fact I shall add another one: When we rejected condescending colonial views of African imitations of Western culture, did we not also deprive ourselves of insights by not considering that these perceptions may have had a core of truth? What I have in mind is the age-old, respectable concept of *mimesis*. As Fritz Kramer's essay (1993) on the subject has shown, Africans, probably long before modern colonization, have employed mimetic modes of confronting and construing alterity that produced, among other things, some of the most striking creations of African visual and performative art.[22] What this means as regards the historical depth of processes we now study as popular culture remains to be explored. The issue of historical depth raises daunting questions I cannot even begin to discuss. Must we not consider the cultures of the African diaspora (maroons in the Caribbean, Afro-Brazilians, African Americans, and other "slave cultures") as contiguous, contemporary expressions, many of which developed on both sides of the Atlantic as a kind of popular culture? (The rise of creole languages, the origins of modern African music, certain religious symbols and practices such as the cults of the mermaid—*mammy wata, yemanja, sirène, madre agua*—are obvious examples.)

Historical depth can also be added to the question of relations between anthropology and popular culture when we consider this: Thinking, talking, and writing, as we seem to do, with the concepts and terms of established high culture, how can we avoid having our inquiries informed by control interests that characterize relations between elitist and popular culture? Such questions evoke dilemmas of anthropological research and writing that may be summarized as follows. Writing—practicing literacy—is always tied to regimes of power. Therefore ethnography—writing about other peoples—is inevitably an exercise of power. How can such a practice serve the aims of critical understanding and liberation from political oppression?[23] A focus on popular culture may lead us to consider the intriguing possibility of approaching this problem from a different perspective. Pressing anthropology into a general scheme of discourses that serve oppression and control in relations between the West and the rest overlooks the specific constellations that exist whenever culture *tout court* is being challenged by popular culture. Much has been made of the complicity of our discipline in colonialism and imperialism; predictably, such deserved criticism is being countered by pointing to anthropology's legitimate descent from the Enlightenment, from which it inherited a "reformatory" (Tylor), critical attitude toward religious bigotry, racism, and cultural provincialism—at least on balance. The present face-off between left and right intellectual positions on almost everything that touches on culture is not likely to promote better understanding of anthropology's role in bringing about developments such as African popular culture.

But what if we were to examine the following hypothesis? Viewed with the benefit of hindsight, based on our current understanding of processes from which popular culture emerged globally, anthropology itself may have to be seen as a practice of the kind we conceptualize as popular culture.[24] Consider the philosophical dilettantism and encyclopedism of our founders, the entrepreneurial approach to publishing "new" systems for mass consumption ("evolutionism" would be an example), the marketing of ethnographic information in popular media from the German *Gartenlaube,* long defunct, to *National Geographic,* very much alive. Add to this a penchant for, and involvement with, expositions, *Völkerschauen* as popular spectacles, such as—to give a French example—the exhibits in the Jardin d'Acclimatation. Take into account the titillation of exotic—and "ancient"—sex, violence, fetishes, and rituals. In short, think of the considerable entertainment value of *ethnologica,* and you get an idea of what I am driving at with my hypothesis. It may be a rude but salutary awakening for our discipline if, after all the time spent, not without success, on gaining academic, high-culture respectability, we were to realize that all along we had our roots, gained our strength, from the same soil from which emerge the ever unruly, vital, and creative movements in music, dance, theater, the visual arts, and literature that we try to catch with the concept of popular culture. All these are but hints and suggestions. Close links between anthropology and popular culture existed (and need to be explored more fully) through the Christian missions and their promotion of a distinctive literature and ethnographic lore for popular consumption. Somewhat esoteric, but nonetheless to the point, were connections between anthropology and spiritism. Of course the search for such connections should not cover only the nineteenth-century beginnings of our discipline. More recently, film and television have been drawing on anthropology, and rapidly developing technologies of interactive learning are likely to increase its contribution to popular entertainment.

Modern mass tourism to the Third World, especially in its educational and philanthropic varieties, also needs to be seen in this light. In fact, we may even have to consider that the practices of empirical research in anthropology we call fieldwork, though ostensibly modeled on habits of collecting and observing that were developed by eighteenth- and nineteenth-century natural history, have in fact been attempts, however halfhearted and clumsy, to "join the dance" of all those movements of survival that our theories classified as acculturation, syncretism, revival, social change, and modernization.[25] Most people still think that what distinguishes anthropology from sociology is that our discipline wants to gain and preserve knowledge of premodern, preindustrial cultures. But the timing alone suggests differently: field research as part of our professionalization did not become obligatory before the first decade or so of this century, *after* the discipline had gained academic recognition. All along, anthropology's coeval subject has been the contemporary world of cultures and societies that had become the targets of Western expansion. Calling what we studied in these societies savage, primitive, tribal, or traditional expressed our wishes, desires (and occasionally orders we received), which we may or may not have shared with the people we encountered in field research. By the time we got to them, the practices of living these cultures and the practices of studying them were interconnected in ways that we suspected only in rare moments.[26]

Why, given all these connections, did it take anthropologists so long to get seriously interested in popular culture[27] and to suspect that popular culture and anthropology might be homologous practices? At least as far as African studies is concerned, one could argue that the decolonization of Africa created the conditions for a decolonization of our minds that made us "discover" popular culture as the fascinating and urgent subject of study we now recognize it to be. Jan Vansina, in a candid reappraisal of his work as an ethnographer, confirms my observations on the blinding effect of the colonial situation:

> It is easy now to see that a description of Kuba institutions and ways of life really made little sense without its colonial context. But even though I myself, like everyone else, was involved all the time in negotiating colonial situations, I simply missed the point. I was blinded by the social anthropology of the day and its emphasis on an atemporal ethnographic present. . . . It would take fifteen years for me to realize fully how efficiently this fiction of an ethnographic present had hidden the workings of the colonial situation. (1994, 27)

At the same time, if anthropology somehow belongs to popular culture, this should lead us to ponder the limits—in fact the eventually self-liquidating nature of popular culture as a discourse distinct from, and opposed to, discourses on elitist and traditional culture. Anthropological studies of popular culture are, or should be, part of the blurring of boundaries between ethnology-anthropology and history (history *tout court,* not just "oral" or ethnohistory). "Historicizing" of our discipline is under way and has changed it at least as profoundly as the "literary turn."

It is perhaps no longer fashionable to speak of imperialism, but who would deny that power is still exercised by societies that are organized as nation-states (though they may be used by multinational business interests) over other societies whose political institutions are shaky and whose economy, if not reduced to subsistence production, is based on exporting cash crops and mineral resources? Reasoning that discourses such as anthropology are oppressive because they are produced by the former and pronounced about the latter once had the simplicity and convincingness that purely referential theories of language maintained as long as we could believe in them. Matters become more complex when we think of anthropology and popular culture together. The idea that anthropology belongs to discourses of power is perhaps not affected by the proposal to think of it as a kind of/part of popular culture. But *how* it serves power becomes an open question. The scenario of collaboration, theoretical and practical, that fit an era of direct colonization may no longer be appropriate. Could it be that anthropology, at least for moments, actually parodies, subverts, and resists imperialism—not so much by intentions or correct political attitudes as by its practices and creations, the way popular culture challenges the powers that be?

The Moral of the Tale

There can be no conclusion to this chapter. Though argumentative at times, it has told of a scholarly journey that, without being planned as such, led to the discovery of popular culture in more than one sense: to the discovery of things, words, and practices previously unnoticed, and to a theoretical frame capable of accommodating these new findings. Keeping in mind that my concerns have been focused on what I found in an urban-industrial context in Zaire during a postcolonial period of almost thirty years, the moral of my tale is this: We need a concept of popular culture. To argue that we can make do with the classical evolutionary distinction between primitive and civilized would amount to something that even the staunchest advocates of Culture with a capital *C* would hesitate to propose. A simple distinction of popular culture as *low culture* as opposed to *high culture* is not worth considering, although such an opposition is often tacitly assumed when contemporary African ways of life are compared with traditional African culture. To call what we are after *folk culture* would be misleading inasmuch as this would commit us to think of its products as folklore. Something as vital and central to contemporary Africa as its popular culture simply does not fit the connotations of quaintness and marginality that folklore carries, certainly in the nontechnical understanding of the term outside the discipline of folklore studies. Nor is there a straight line of descent from *Volkskultur* discovered in the nineteenth century (or for that matter from the distinction between great and little traditions that informed so much anthropological work, especially in Latin America) to what we now conceptualize as popular culture. Its contemporaneity demands that we pay attention to concerns such as commoditization, mass media, mass consumption, and globalization. No one engaged in the study of popular culture can ignore these issues, though it is equally true that what we try to catch with the theory of popular culture cannot be reduced to any one of them. *Mass culture,* to continue our list of possible candidates, is too broad; *workers' culture* is too narrow, and so is *urban or industrial culture.* All of these designations suggest only some aspects of processes that need to be studied in their African specificity and may or may not converge with what the terms denote in Europe or North America. *Counterculture* wouldn't be bad, because it does catch a characteristic of African popular culture, but it is again disqualified by its specific, narrow connotations (youth, drugs, new religions) in Euramerican societies.

All this is not to say I am about to advocate a parochial concept of popular culture tailored to ethnographic research in Shaba. What I have in mind is ultimately the claim that popular culture forces us to rethink the idea of culture itself. If I had to describe the decisive theoretical consequences, or at any rate the concomitants, of a turn to popular culture, I would name four.

First, the concept of popular culture enables us to think about culture not only in the plural but as in itself plural. Moral authority and constraints, rational consistency and purpose (all of this supported by clearly defined roles and institutions) were once projected onto culture as a system. Such a view must give way to considering culture a praxis that also entails contradiction, contestation, and experimentation; in short, negativity and freedom.

Second, popular culture cannot be thought of as a quasi-timeless symbolic chart of common representations marking well-defined spaces of identity. Instead, it encourages us to conceive of cultural practices as creative expressions and joint performances in shared time. More than that, shared time is also recognized as the condition of studying and understanding popular culture, which can only be experienced as contemporaneous and contemporary. Popular culture is of and in the same time as the anthropologist's culture.

Third, it follows from these premises that inquiries into popular culture have a political dimension; relations of power need to be considered not just as imposed by colonial imperialism but as inherent in cultural processes that are predicated as much on freedom and confrontation as on norms and integration.

For my fourth observation I need to back up briefly. The classical conception envisaged culture as hovering somewhere above the world of needs and necessities. Therefore the study of material conditions tended to be relegated to biology and economics. When questions of interdependence or determination arose they divided theoreticians into hostile tribes of, for instance, symbolic anthropologists and cultural materialists. We now begin to realize that both positions could be upheld only because idealists and materialists alike had thoroughly abstract visions of culture as an object of research. Thought about popular culture has if not brought about, then certainly encouraged inquiries into the materiality of culture. True, concern for the body and embodiment may have had other origins (for instance, in gender studies). The rehabilitation of the senses proclaimed against visualism was proposed for epistemological reasons; material culture, long a marginal subdiscipline, has seen a remarkable theoretical revival in recent years. But all the considerations above can and must be brought together when we take up the study of popular culture.

Although popular culture liberates us from elitist, hierarchical, and integrative thought about culture, it does not do away with the deepest and most encompassing problem that any theory of culture raises or hides, as the case may be: How should we think about confrontations between us and them, self and other, Occident and Orient, the West and the rest? There is an obvious overlap between popular culture and what we perceive as the reemergence of ethnicity, regionalism, and nationalism, where hope and horror, creating and killing seem to be blend in ways that defy rational analysis. Work on popular culture has become a very serious game indeed.

"There is a crack, a crack in everything, that's how the light gets in," says the popular poet and singer Leonard Cohen. The theory of popular culture is a way to reveal or open cracks in received culture theory. Our aim should be to formulate insights and come up with findings that make the adjective "popular" unnecessary. If and when this happens, it may turn out that we don't need the noun "culture" either. But that is perhaps too much to hope for.

In the meantime, I think both theorizing about popular culture and doing empirical research on it should be guided by a few simple questions: When we employ the concept, what does it lump, bring together, that the classical concept of culture is incapable of joining? What does popular culture separate or distinguish that culture *tout court* lumps together? What comes to mind here is above all the antagonism, the contradictions, and the play of power that an integrationist concept of culture tends to cover rather than reveal. It will take time and the work of researchers who are now starting out to answer a last, disquieting question. By now we know pretty well what we catch with the concept of popular culture, but what do we miss?

Meanwhile . . . and Elsewhere: A Bibliographical Note

I never started out with a theory of popular culture. When I thought I needed one I formulated my own programmatic statement ad hoc (Fabian 1978), without the benefit of wide reading on the subject. That paper still describes the orientation I use in current work. When, in the early 1980s a plan to organize, with Peter

Burke and others, an interdisciplinary symposium on popular culture had to be abandoned for lack of funding, I turned to specific projects, setting aside generalizing reflections until I had to think about these essays. I still have no ambition to take on the literature on the subject. But precisely because I will follow my own train of thought, I should offer a few observations on how my work relates to the current state of debate.[28]

As far as I can see, most of the elements of current debates were assembled by the mid- or late seventies (see, for instance, Poujol and Labourie 1979; closely related issues were discussed at the same time under the heading "working-class culture," for instance, Clarke, Critcher, and Johnson 1979). A trend that was visible then has become more pronounced through the years: different national interests have produced different discourses, a topic that is addressed and exemplified in the important work on contemporary bourgeois culture by Orval Löfgren (e.g., 1989). Therefore, when browsing through works that deal with popular culture one finds only partial overlap and sometimes none at all. In Germany, for instance, even a pioneering study such as Bausinger's (1986), critical of an ahistorical conception of folklore and *Volkskultur,* cannot escape a heritage of thought that makes issues such as authenticity central (addressing topics such as kitsch that are all but ignored in recent writings on mass culture). In the United States popular culture is (almost) synonymous with mass media culture. To me this is exemplified by a book I picked up eagerly and put down with considerable disappointment: a study titled *Popular Culture Genres* that appeared in the series Foundations of Popular Culture (Berger 1992). On the other hand, I was both impressed and made uneasy when I read Greil Marcus's remarkable *Lipstick Traces: A Secret History of the Twentieth Century* (1989). He takes an approach to popular music (rock and punk) that is similar to some of the most interesting work on popular religion (especially on its continuity with hermetic traditions). Construing a kind of parallel, almost conspiratorial, history for popular culture, Marcus's approach makes it possible to celebrate the challenge popular culture puts forth while at the same time containing that challenge in a "secret history." To reserve for popular culture its own history, as it were, is a temptation we must resist. Popular culture study is not antiestablishment just because of its subject.

When I had convinced myself that the American perspective on popular culture was probably furthest removed from the one that has been guiding my own work, I came upon George Lipsitz's *Time Passages* (1990). Lipsitz offers convincing arguments against excluding anything from popular culture just because it is mass-produced, and he comes to conclusions about collective memory and the recuperation of history in popular culture that are quite similar to my own. Incidentally, with a remark (a tantalizing hint, really) on the common origins of his discipline, history, and commercialized leisure, the distinctive form of popular culture he studies (1990, 5), he points in the same direction as my observations on homologies between anthropology and popular culture.

In spite of a seemingly ever increasing diversity of interests and approaches that has made the concept at the same time fashionable and all but unmanageable, popular culture has shown remarkable staying power. As some of the recent work I found most interesting shows, this may be due to the growing realization that definitions and theoretical schemes are of limited value in understanding what might be called the historicity of popular culture, as well as the historicity of any possible discourse about popular culture. In other words, studies of popular culture are valuable to the extent that they make visible their own genesis.

The history of the term and concept as a history of its uses is explored by Morag Shiach (1989). Though its orientation is mainly literary and British, I would recommend her study as an excellent introduction to discourses on popular culture. She begins with a critical analysis of the entry "popular" in the *Oxford English Dictionary* and then applies her findings in a series of essays on topics ranging from peasant poets in the eighteenth and nineteenth centuries to contemporary television. Shiach touches, as far as I can see, on most of the issues I have discussed in this chapter or will take up later.[29] She also makes a convincing effort to explain the absence of women from accounts of popular culture (9): "Women disappear from accounts of popular culture as a result of particular methodological preoccupations and practices. They are also constantly marginalized in narratives of popular culture. Critics offer 'popular culture' as heroic narrative of authenticity and coherence vs. triviality and decay. Such a narrative must have a hero, who is, of course, male" (13).[30] Although this absence comes in degrees, I have been aware of it in others' work as well as my own. In my case it is too late now to remedy this on the side of research; there will be some reflection, though, on what Shiach calls "methodological preoccupations and practices."

One of the most encompassing attempts to discern popular culture as a subject shared by history, anthropology, sociology, and cultural criticism is a reader edited by Chandra Mukerji and Michael Schudson (1991). Their approach has its merits in that it creates interesting links within a wide range of writing, but I have difficulty recognizing anthropology's road to popular culture in the contributions that appear in the section devoted to our discipline.

William Rowe and Vivian Schelling's *Memory and Modernity* (1991) is a work whose orientation I found congenial. They too point out that to "call something popular carries an implied opposition" (2). They criticize both romantic valuation of "authentic rural culture under threat from industrialization" and modern conceptions equating popular culture with mass culture, then adopt a third position that they trace to "Marx and beyond" and that "ascribes to popular culture an emancipatory and utopian charge, whereby the practices of the oppressed classes contain within them resources for imagining an alternative future society" (2).

Both Shiach and Rowe and Schelling draw on Antonio Gramsci's notion of hegemony when it comes to understanding how popular culture is involved in relations of power.[31] I especially like Rowe and

Schelling's suggestion that "one way of developing [Gramsci's] insights is to take popular culture not as a given view of the world but as a space or series of spaces where popular subjects, as distinct from members of ruling groups, are formed" (1991, 10). A little later they spell out one of the consequences: "When the popular is defined not as an object, a meaning or a social group, but as a site—or, more accurately, a series of dispersed sites [here is an echo from Foucault]—then it generates a principle of opposition to the idea, imposed by authoritarian liberalism or by populism, of the nation as single body" (ibid.). They too argue that to "place the relationships between dominant power and the popular inside a vocabulary of conformity versus resistance entails simplification and distortion" (11). This assertion (with a focus on resistance studies in general) is further developed in a comprehensive critical essay by Sherry Ortner (1995), and I will back it up with ethnographic evidence in the next chapter.

Like others, I find it hard to resist using James C. Scott's imaginative and accurate phrase when I think and talk about the broader political significance of various expressions of popular culture: these are indeed "weapons of the weak." I also like his list of everyday forms of resistance: "foot dragging, dissimulation, desertion, false compliance, pilfering, feigned ignorance, slander, arson, sabotage, and so on" (Scott 1985, xvi).[32] I admire the close ethnographic attention he paid to such manifestations of a "venerable popular culture of resistance" (xvii) as well as the general contribution his book makes to the debate on resistance. At the same time, we should not forget that Scott's study focused on peasants. It will become clear that inquiries into urban resistance often face different challenges, among them formidable problems of scale. How can one reasonably generalize from ethnographic research conducted in cities with populations that range from 200,000 to perhaps 850,000? Such problems would be unmanageable if it were not for the emergence of popular culture as a vast array of mediations of experience—embodiments, objects, practices, texts, images—that are shared by the masses and are the access routes individual researchers can take. This is why my list of forms of resistance, though Scott's enumeration fits my findings, also includes religious dissent and innovation, pop music, theater, genre painting, historiography, "and so on."

The two aspects of mediation I referred to—lived experience and research—are dealt with admirably in a book that, though the term hardly ever occurs in it, is one of the most compelling studies of popular culture (*and* of anthropology in a contemporary urban context) I have come across recently: James Siegel's *Solo in the New Order* (1986). Siegel's book invites comparison with a pioneering anthropological study of popular theater that should also be mentioned here, James Peacock's *Rites of Modernization* (1968), written under the then reigning paradigm of culturalism whose power and limits it illustrates.

I should at least mention the relevance to popular culture studies of the work on "everyday life," developed especially in France, and acknowledge inspiration from, among others, the writings of Michel de Certeau (1984), especially his essay "Reading as Poaching" in the volume cited. Interest in the quotidian and the theoretical reasons that make the quotidian interesting is beginning to produce outstanding studies on work and leisure in colonial towns in Africa. Hansen (1989), White (1990), and Martin (1995) are examples. Martin's work especially, about Kinshasa's sister city Brazzaville, is a rich source for the origins of popular culture on both sides of the Congo. Regional surveys are beginning to appear (Graebner 1992), but except for certain forms of expression such as music, painting, or theater, I am not aware of writings on popular culture dealing with Africa as a whole.

Feelings that the concept I have been proposing may be, after all, too much tailored to Third World circumstances will be dispelled by the theoretical convergences I found in a remarkable historical essay on the Viennese operetta and its origins in the multicultural world of the Habsburg empire (Csáky 1996, a book I hope will soon be available in English). By way of lateral association, this brings up the notion of an urban cultural scene, a concept that may prove useful in localizing centers of the production of contemporary African culture. "Scene" guides a documentary exploration of cultural creativity in Lagos (Brockmann and Hötter 1994), which in a similar form could also be conducted in other African capitals.

When I think about important readings on the subject of popular culture, I must at least include a global reference to the ethnography of speaking or communication (which, in a more technical incarnation, may be called interactive sociolinguistics; Hymes 1974). At its best, it laid the foundations for the kind of theory of popular culture I have been circumscribing in this essay: it freed us from an essentially referential theory of language (and by extension, of culture) and opened up a vast field of inquiries into the pragmatics of culture (giving concepts such as performance their deserved place next to, and beyond, signification, meaning, orientation, and motivation). As a conscious critique of formalist linguistics, decidedly high culture and text oriented, this was certainly a movement of popular resistance (one of those homologies between anthropology and popular culture I speculated about earlier). It signaled and promoted convergence between the anthropology of contemporary everyday life and folklore studies, sometimes to the point that the two are distinguished only by institutional divisions. For an early, important example see the collection of papers edited by Dan Ben-Amos (1976; originally published in the journal *Genre* in 1969 and 1971). The relevance of this theoretical trend to popular culture studies is also clear in the work of Richard Bauman (1977, 1986) and especially in the recent study by Elizabeth Tonkin (1992).

Finally, I want to recommend the essays by Ngũgĩ wa Thiong'o in his *Moving the Centre: The Struggle for Cultural Freedoms* (1993). They provide an African insider's counterpoint as well as a "universalist" approach to contemporary African culture, a perspective outsider specialists should strive to attain.

2

✧ ✧ ✧

Power Within: Genres in Popular Culture

In its acknowledged capacity to organize resistance to abusive (or intrusive) power, popular culture draws on or invents various genres of representation and performance. What about the notion of genre itself? Genre is a concept of wide, if diffuse, popularity whose cognitive or aesthetic meaning is seldom extended to include relations of power (other than the power of critics who pronounce on generic rules and qualities). Anthropological studies of popular culture can contribute to the discussion by showing how genre works when it does work, what it accomplishes, and what it prevents. From my own first experiment with genre as part of a theory of cultural emergence, I learned that the concept makes us aware of contradictions calling for resolution: although genre empowers, it may also be experienced as overpowering; genre enables, genre constrains. Looking at concrete situations and cases can teach us that these seemingly contradictory qualities are not divided between the powerful and the powerless. In other words, when we raise the question of power in our exploration of popular culture, reaction or resistance to domination is not the only issue to be addressed, or even the most significant. Otherwise we would have to assume that popular culture is essentially pseudomorphous, having its specific forms determined by the shapes of power it must resist or accommodate to rather than by what it invents.

Genre and Power

"Genre," derived from the Latin *genus* (whose root is shared by many other terms such as general, but also "gender" and "generation"), is not part of the vocabulary we use in most of our ordinary conversations. Still, for educated speakers of languages within the sphere of Latin, it is well nigh impossible to avoid encounters with it, if only in formulaic expressions such as "this is not his genre" (probably, and significantly, most often voiced in this negative form). If we were to question users of the word about the genre of terms "genre" belongs to, the response would most likely be that it occurs in talk about literature or art. Novels are a genre of writing; they have seen or heard about exhibitions of genre painting; they have read the term in music or film reviews. Most of our respondents would probably also be aware that being able to name and discuss genres shows that one recognizes differences and relations between products of culture. If we were to probe further, we would find that at least some people are aware of conceptual connections between genre and the root term *genus*. Ah yes, *genus* and *species*—we all were taught at least the rudiments of Aristotelian logic and biological classification. Already we are enveloped in a rather dark cloud of connotations that leaves us feeling a chill in the air, a kind of threat. Genre—much like value, norm, standard—embodies cultural injunctions to know what belongs and what doesn't, what is proper and what isn't, what is well crafted and what is bricolage.

The purpose of this rapid reflection on genre was to fill in a background we presumably share before the discussion gets more technical. I wanted to show that even casual reflection on the concept leads us to notions and practices that are central to our culture (central in the sense that they demand, and command, more respect than others) and that, if we were pressed to state the principal meaning of genre, we would say that it expresses concern with evaluation as well as classification and taxonomy, hence with norms and order.

Now if we combine these two insights—let's say that genre has to do with authority and order—we inevitably also evoke power: power exercised through acts of distinction and imposition, and power suffered through denial of recognition and through submission to criteria of distinction.[1]

Power Within

Anthropology and Genre Research

Fortunately, as an anthropologist I cannot be expected to address the question of power and genre in the vast field of literary theory and criticism.[2] Unfortunately, cultural anthropology has become so permeable to literary theory that it is impossible to plead ignorance. In the absence of disciplinary boundaries that protect us (not only from literary theorizing but also from linguistic, psychological, economic, biological, and a few other kinds), we do well to remember our special role within the academic division of labor. Although we cannot stake out a territory—and constantly less so as the world becomes "global"—our history and research practices entitle us to claim a focus, a center of attention: anthropology is about otherness. Simply to say that anthropology is the study of other cultures would be contested by disciplines that also study other cultures (geography, history, political science, etc.) and by anthropologists who study their own cultures. The former usually do not make otherness a theme, the latter don't have to; struggle with otherness has produced most of the theories and methods that qualify their work as anthropological. Of course anthropological knowledge is not just a catalog of differences; we try to work out what other cultures *are like*. Still, in the end it is difference that gives significance to our substantive findings. And that also goes for what anthropologists might have to say about genre and popular culture.

When we approach *other cultures* with or through the notion of genre, we face a quandary: How can a concept that manifestly embodies values central to our own culture be made to serve the production of knowledge about other cultures, knowledge that amounts to more than projection at best and subsumption at worst? Put somewhat differently, Is it possible to make inquiries into genres and generic distinctions other than *by operating* (as opposed to questioning, examining) generic distinctions? Or put in yet another way, Can we investigate generic distinctions without reproducing what we already know? Of course we can. We could operate our criteria and standards and then find out whether other cultures recognize and distinguish genres, be they novels, portrait paintings, sonatas, or horror movies. Of course we cannot. Although this would provide us with comparative material that has been grist for anthropological mills for a long time, we have all but abandoned the paradigm within which comparisons of this sort made sense: evolutionism. At least I don't know of any anthropologists at present studying genre whose work is guided, consciously, by evolutionary schemes.

To imagine concretely what I meant by hinting at mindless reproduction of our own categories, one need only recall what folklore studies was like between its interesting romantic origins and its recent theoretical revival: one of the most deadeningly positivistic disciplines engaged in collecting and classifying specimens of lore for the purpose of construing taxonomies that competed with those used in zoology or botany. But things have changed. Many folklorists and anthropologists are now engaged in genre research that is virtually indistinguishable, and both have recourse to literary theory. The consensus seems to be that genre is too interesting and important a subject of research to be put off until the quandary just described is resolved.[3]

Genre and Power in Popular Culture

Genre and Power: The Jamaa Religious Movement

My entry into the urban-industrial world of Shaba was through the study of the Jamaa, a religious movement among Catholic mission Christians. In 1966–67 I spent eighteen months doing field research in Shaba (then still called Katanga). Most of the time I lived in Kolwezi and in the workers' town of Musonoi near that city; for shorter periods I visited groups in Likasi and Lubumbashi (then still called Jadotville and Elisabethville) and took several trips upcountry and along the railroad to the Angolan border. Briefly,[4] the Jamaa was founded in 1953 by Placide Tempels, a Belgian missionary who then worked near the mining town of Kolwezi. Membership was (with few exceptions) restricted to married couples, recruited at first from among the mine and railway workers who lived in the principal urban centers and along the railroad. The Jamaa could be described as an elaboration and ritualization of ideas Tempels had first formulated in his famous *Bantu Philosophy*.[5] The movement was lay centered; members of the clergy could join but attained leadership only when they were recognized for their charismatic authority. Members were expected to be totally committed to Jamaa teaching and ritual and at the same time to participate in an exemplary way in the ritual life of the Catholic Church. The Jamaa refrained from political action in the narrow sense of the word but was from the beginning perceived as a problem by the church and, given their close collaboration with the church, by the management of the mining company and the colonial (and postcolonial) authorities.

The approach I took to the Jamaa was informed by Max Weber's theory of charisma. Interest in emerging authority and power, one could say, went with that approach (though Weber wasn't Foucault). Strange as this may seem now, because this Weberian view of charisma was enveloped, as it were, in culture theory that was then at its most culturalist stage of development, it did not lead me to make power a central topic. Nor did I take much care to place this workers' movement in a larger scheme of colonial labor history. My attention was riveted, and stayed riveted for years to come, on the Jamaa's particular doctrine and organization that made it such an interesting case for the study of cultural creativity and innovation.[6]

How did I get to genre? I was still in the midst of fieldwork when I began groping for a start, a first ethnographic report. I decided to publish a paper on leadership and dream interpretation (Fabian 1966), based on recorded exchanges with several leaders of the movement. Dreaming was firmly established in the movement as a communicative praxis, and the interpretation of dreams—involving an assessment of content and timing in relation to the movement's teachings and rites of initiation—was an important source of charismatic authority for members who occupied high positions in the lineages of spiritual descent that were the main organizational structure of the Jamaa. As work progressed and texts accumulated, the question of charismatic authority receded into the background; my main concern became the charismatic message (designated by the term *mawazo,* thoughts): the pronouncements of the founder and his followers, the system of doctrinal terms and their logic, and the practices of transmitting and internalizing the doctrine (Fabian 1971). I had tried out what was then one of the most promising avenues of a "new ethnography"—the idea that culture was, first of all and fundamentally, concerned with cognition and that *a* culture could best be described as a lexicon of labels / terms exhibiting characteristic taxonomic arrangements of concepts / terms. Noticing the obvious—that doctrine was not taught, let alone practiced, in systems of terms but was part of communicative exchanges—and having accumulated a corpus of texts produced in such exchanges, I moved from classifying terms to interpreting texts. This meant I now found myself in a situation similar to that of a folklorist who tries to get a grip on a body of oral lore by distinguishing genres and classifying texts. As it happened, I had lost faith in, and pleasure with, taxonomic games.

At the same time, I had become disillusioned with the view that took culture to be a blueprint or template for social action. I needed a theory of culture as communicative praxis, for which I found inspiration and guidance in up-and-coming sociolinguistics, above all in Dell Hymes's proposals for an "ethnography of communication."[7] The result was an attempt to present Jamaa doctrine, its content, the form of its expressions, and its structures of authority and power as a process of differentiation of genres. The movement established and reproduced itself in a system—now I would say a discourse or regime—of authoritatively defined speech events. These events came in kinds (I distinguished five)[8] whose most conspicuous property was their repetitiveness or recursiveness. They were either named by the movement or otherwise consistently referred to in descriptive phrases (see Fabian 1974; reprinted in Fabian 1991, chap. 3).

As regards the role of power in developing and maintaining this particular set of genres, two things were immediately noticeable. Genres were crucial in defining the movement's identity vis-à-vis the mission church, the background from which it had come and from which, for a long time, it refused to be separated. But they also distinguished it from other religious movements that had emerged and found their followers at about the same time, in the same region and social class.[9] From the beginning of the movement, we could say, genre was involved with power by giving form to resistance to, or defiance of, Catholic hierarchical authority and by marking distinction from, if not competition with, other organized expressions of religious enthusiasm.

At the time, however, connections between power and genre were even more conspicuous inside the movement. Communicative competence, expressed in mastering the genres of teaching, counseling, and dream interpretation, clearly was the basis of authority and leadership. Outteaching each other in an effort to outdo each other with proofs of spiritual fecundity became a more or less open form of power struggle in a movement that stressed unity and mutual love as equally central. Generic strictures put checks on these potentially disruptive tendencies; struggle for power (short of schism, which also occurred) had to respect the rules that made genres vehicles of power and authority.

Just how much the movement was preoccupied with power is revealed indirectly by one of the most interesting features of Jamaa discourse and interaction. Institutionalized in the system and strongly reinforced as part of initiation ritual, the Jamaa had developed a genre of communication referred to as encounter (*rencontre, mapatano*), an emotionally charged exchange of deep thoughts and aspirations, usually between an initiating couple and the couple to be initiated. Thus a discourse and practice of self-effacement and humiliation and a kind of spiritual (and allegedly often carnal) coupling through self-revelation formed the core of the movement. Of course the utopian idea of power-free encounter confirmed concern with power by its (temporary) negation. The self-humiliation (*kujishusha*) that such encounter required was valued not so much as a moral virtue, but as an act of social and political negation. "Encounter," which included humiliation and self-effacement, was initially proclaimed by the founder as the way to overcome his own separation, based on his race and his place in the colonial hierarchy, from the people he was supposed to convert to Christianity. In Jamaa discourse this idea was preserved, although emphasis shifted to inequalities of gender and socioeconomic status and to the divisions caused by "tribalism." In sum, the idea of encounter (which, incidentally, connected the Jamaa to many other encounter movements around the world and thereby to an emerging global culture)[10] can be understood as part of a discourse concerned with power, not only by its logic (that is, its being an affirmation of a state of affairs by—temporary—negation) but above all by its institutionalization as a genre within a system of genres of communication.

Although this may seem to have little bearing on the issue of genre and power, we should take another look at the rule, mentioned earlier, that only couples could become members of the Jamaa. One is tempted to say it is explained by the logic of initiation through encounter, but such an argument would be circular. That it should be *married* couples has usually been put down to Catholicism, from which members were recruited; married meant married in the church and was recognized by the civil authorities as a legal state different from "customary marriage." Most Christian couples continued to make customary arrangements, usually symbolized by exchanges of gifts as well as payments in kind or cash. These arrangements were tolerated by the mission and actively encouraged by the management of the mining company as safeguards for the stability of marital unions. The name Jamaa itself ("family" in Shaba Swahili) initially caused outsiders to perceive the movement as one of many similar organizations that were part of the mission-sponsored *mouvement familial*. The latter, with close links to Catholic workers' and youth organizations, aimed at strengthening the nuclear family, which also happened to be one of the means chosen by government and company policies of "stabilizing" a self-reproductive labor force. Tempels, who was certainly aware of the role the Catholic missions played in implementing colonial labor policy, liked to support his teachings with examples from Luba culture. He would remind his listeners (at that time mostly first-generation immigrants to the cities) of traditional pacts of faithfulness between spouses creating mutual obligations that went beyond what was customary, or of initiation into hunters' societies that required involvement of the hunter's wife. Did he know that his urban followers, whom he imagined torn between tradition and imported Christianity, had other contexts and models for thought about "modern" male-female relations? By the early fifties, Congolese popular music had made gender and marriage relations a major topic, as well as a pervasive metaphor for relations of political and economic power (more about this in chapter 4). There is no reason to believe that Jamaa followers were less exposed to the influence of the great singer-poets of the time than the general population who lived in the cities, where record players and radios were never silent. Was Tempels aware of popular music, and how did he react to it? Quite likely he shared with other colonials a disdain for "Congo jazz." As far as my own awareness is concerned, the theoretical approach I took in my work made me blind, or rather deaf, to that part of the movement's world. I had as yet given little or no thought to popular culture.

Genre and Power: Popular Painting in Shaba

In 1972 I returned to Shaba, this time with a project on language and labor, initially conceived as a study of Shaba Swahili in the context of industrial and artisanal work. Gradually I came to understand that the practices I was studying were part of an encompass-

1. *Mermaid,* a key symbol of popular culture in Zaire (painted by Louis Kalema, Lubumbashi, 1974); from the author's collection.

ing workers' culture. The latter soon became the focus of research, leading to a shift from a more narrowly defined sociolingistic approach to inquiries into expressions of popular culture. This led to a discovery that eventually overshadowed other concerns. It began with my noticing the picture of a mermaid in the house of some Jamaa people I was visiting (fig. 1). This was my first glimpse at what turned out to be a vast production of paintings for local consumption. The artists were mostly self-taught; they worked with locally available materials and sold their work at a small profit. As a rule, they had to paint and sell at least one picture a day to make a modest living. They found their customers in places of commerce and entertainment and, above all, among those members of the local population who, in the ways they arranged and decorated their domestic living space, expressed their aspirations to a petit bourgeois lifestyle. Cautious estimates for the city of Lubumbashi alone (population ca. 850,000 at that time) put the volume of this production-consumption at about ten thousand paintings offered and sold per year. Incidentally, though consumption is a handy term, especially if paired with production, it has its problems in describing popular painting as a social practice. As objects, these paintings were not consumed, literally or figuratively. No one would have put them into the category of relatively durable consumer goods like refrigerators, cars, or television sets. The paintings themselves meant very little to their owners (who would easily discard and perhaps replace those that had deteriorated or been eaten away by termites); having pictures around when times came "to remember" was what made people keep and display these objects (more about this below). As far as can be told, genre paintings were never resold or even given away (except to the few foreign collectors who began to get interested in genre painting not long before it disappeared again in the late seventies).

As the material accumulated—samples of the work, recorded conversations with painters, surveys of use—it turned out that the artists and their customers shared conceptions not only of the function of these paintings, but also of their content and meaning. They consistently defined the domain by a criterion of inclusion they called *ukumbusho,* a picture's capacity to activate memory and reflection (the term is derived from a causative form of the verb *-kumbuka,* whose meaning is somewhere between "to remember" and "to think"). Within that domain, a limited, albeit never strictly defined, number of kinds of pictures were distinguished, almost always by commonly known labels. These were produced and sold in great quantities. It was this feature of a process of creating and maintaining a domain of discourse and representation through internal differentiation in terms of distinctive and repetitive realizations (rather than a certain overall resemblance of the pictures to what has been called genre painting in art history) that led me to consider once again the notion of genre.

I was struck by certain formal analogies that seemed to obtain between the constitution, through internal differentiation, of a religious tradition represented in texts that could be distinguished in terms of genres and the emergence of an artistic tradition represented in paintings whose production and consumption showed similar properties of distinction and recursiveness.

This is not the place to show that relationship in detail or to explore how generic analysis worked in the case of popular painting.[11] The question in this chapter is what genres in popular culture can tell us about power. In the case of the charismatic movement, the significance of power, at least in general terms, was implicit in the sociological approach to charismatic authority. Matters were less obvious with popular painting. Still, the following can be said without projecting mere ideas onto the material or overinterpreting what paintings and texts show. The domain, the "what" of popular painting, being defined as *ukumbusho,* is (shared) memories, or better (remembering the causative form of the Swahili term), a practice of calling up memories. Simplifying what is in fact a much more complex matter, one could say that the artists represented shared memory in objects that were, for their viewers, reminders, often literally prompts, for narratives. Popular painting, in other words, had a pragmatic as well as a semiotic function. Given the exposure of much of the adult population in the early seventies to colonization in the past and to a totalitarian regime in the present, it was not surprising that the memories that attained generic status were those that gave striking expression to experiences with the powers that be: many paintings depicted oppression, exploitation, violence suffered, poverty endured, and inequality resented. Ancestral life under powerful chiefs, the Arab slave trade, the colonial penal system, suffering inflicted by the upheavals of independence and secession, and incomprehensible accumulation of wealth in the hands of a few were among the most popular genres of Shaba painting; so were struggles for power among politicians, acts of resistance, armed rebellions, and their repression. Also appreciated were genres that encouraged and condensed reflection on the nature of power, on achievements of survival, as well as on enjoying a measure of the good life.

When we want to assess the relation of power and genre in Shaba painting, it is not enough to show that most pictures *represent* one or the other aspect of power exercised or power suffered. The question that needs to be addressed is how generic differentiation itself may relate to power. An answer, it seems to me, suggests itself when we look back for a moment at what I found in the Jamaa movement. There it was generic differentiation that constituted a domain of discourse as well as a distinctive religious practice. In the case of painting, shared memory was structured through distinct themes or topics whose generic reproduction doubled the effects of narration: every popular painting from Shaba was narrative according to art-historical criteria. But beyond that, every generic picture was capable of evoking "the whole story," or at any rate a narrative that is more encompassing than what the picture represents. Artists could survive only as long as they guessed correctly what kind of theme had attained generic status and was therefore in popular demand. This was a two-way process that engaged painters and their customers in reflection and critical exchanges. In short, popular painting not only produced images of power, it created, within the overall practice of popular culture, a space of freedom from control by government or by the special interests pursued by large employers and the missions.[12]

The overall similarity that appears to characterize what I have said so far about genre and power in the Jamaa movement and in Shaba popular painting has to be weighed against significant differences. To begin with, as discourses, Jamaa *mawazo* and popular *ukumbusho* differed in their degrees of closure and in their criteria for admittance. Jamaa teaching has been exclusive; the movement's doctrine was clearly defined (a trait that was reinforced rather than weakened by heterodoxy and schism), and participation in its practices demanded specific rituals of initiation. Shaba painting rested on a system of memory whose outer limits and internal structures could be specified at a given moment but were neither dependent on nor maintained by criteria of orthodoxy. The market exercised certain constraints on participation, but only as far as possessing and displaying pictures went. Consequently, Jamaa *mawazo* and popular *ukumbusho* differed considerably in how far they were penetrated by—in fact depended on and interacted with—other domains of popular culture such as storytelling, music, and other performance practices, notably popular theater. Another difference appears when we compare the content and intent of the respective discourses. Jamaa teaching has been religious and philosophical, with mystic and perhaps gnostic overtones. Painting was decidedly secular, narrative-historical, and political. It was therefore socially more encompassing.[13]

Genre and Boundaries

I spoke of Jamaa genres of communication and of the representations of shared memories in genre painting as "systems." It is impossible to use that term without conjuring up connotations of linguistic-semiotic structuralism or sociological structuralism-functionalism. In modern anthropology these theoretical approaches have, as competing paradigms, been engaged in debates whose clamor tended to hide the fact that feuding schools shared an integrationist concept of culture, including the injunction that, as a system, culture should be, as Talcott Parsons liked to put it, "boundary maintaining." Postmodern revisions made this criterion a prime target of attack, with results that on the whole have been salutary inasmuch as they demolished monolithic images of culture. Yet the counterimages of pluralism, multivocality, playfulness, and anarchy should not lead us to ignore boundaries and exclusion in cultural practices where they exist, including those that occur in popular culture. These issues are obviously relevant in any attempt to assess the role of power, and they should be raised with respect to the way genre works in our two ethnographic examples.

But first a word about the theoretical background. Much has been said and written recently about the play of power that is set in motion by ethnographic inquiries. The idea of the ethnographer as a distanced observer, already modified by the concept of participant observation (a diffuse notion without an exact referent but open to unlimited connotations), has given way to revisions that conceive of research as dialogue. There are, in current debates, "soft" (often ethical, if not moralizing) and "hard" (epistemological) ways of thinking about dialogue. They oscillate between realizing what is good and considering what is necessary for the production of ethnographic knowledge. The latter position (which may include the former) is based on the insight that ethnography is a communicative practice. There can be no doubt that such a view makes available to anthropology a wide array of critical concepts and procedures that have a bearing on objectivity and the validation of knowledge. But to declare that ethnography is communication has certain intrinsic problems (because its significance obviously depends on what is conceived of as communication as well as on how much of cultural practice can be qualified as communication).[14] Above all, emphasis on communication does not dispose of the problem of power relations.

During my field research on the Jamaa, there were numerous occasions when genre, by setting boundaries, would control what was said to whom and in what manner; none was more vexing and at times painful than the refusal by Jamaa leaders and members to engage in conversation about the movement with me, let alone submit to interviews, however unstructured. This was not a trivial case of caginess or lack of rapport. Nor should one attribute this reticence to the rule of secrecy that was said to govern most of the movement's teaching and initiatory rites, putting refusal to talk down to a quasi-universal penchant among religious cults for the esoteric and hermetic. Such an interpretation would be an essentialist shortcut. The interesting question about secrecy is not *what it actually hides* of the content of a doctrine, or of the actions of a ritual, but *how it affects practices of communication.*

Lack of comprehension also does not account for the Jamaa's refusal to engage in free exchange. Tempels's followers understood the nature of my work. In the mid-sixties, many of those I met had known the founder personally and had participated in his ethnographic search for a "Bantu philosophy." I was well introduced, and with few exceptions I was treated with genuine warmth and sympathy. At first it probably helped that I could talk little and had to listen a lot until I became reasonably fluent in Shaba Swahili. Then (and also in later years) we spent countless hours talking, but always within the generic boundaries of Jamaa discourse that did not include conversation or responding to questions whenever the movement itself was even remotely touched on[15] (which, given the degree of identification charismatic enthusiasm requires, included practically all but the most mundane subjects). Whether I asked for permission to record our exchanges made no difference. Even without the tape recorder present, I would be *taught* about the Jamaa (genre *mafundisho*), perhaps counseled in matters of practicing the teachings (genre *mashaurio*), sometimes invited to share my deep thoughts (genre testimony/*mapatano*).

In sum, any kind of communication that was not also an enactment of an accepted genre was refused, usually in such a way that my interlocutors would turn the tables on me, telling *me* to listen or respond to *their* questions (questions, that is, that were part of teaching). I grew up as an ethnographer—because this was my first training as a researcher—with few doubts about powers of resistance to power exercised by Western scientific practice. Through the years these experiences have caused me to argue for radical revisions of the received prescription of participant observation that, no matter how much stress was put on participation, held to a positivist conception of ethnography as essentially observation. Sometimes I feared that my specific experience with the Jamaa might have unduly colored my ideas of ethnography as communication in a field of power relations. It was exciting to read Jan Vansina's recollections of his fieldwork among the Kuba in the (still colonial) fifties. Although he does not put it in terms of generic constraints, his relations with his interlocutors were much like those

I found in the Jamaa. In his autobiographic account, Vansina comes, post factum, to conclusions regarding the nature of ethnography that have informed positions he seems to distrust as "postmodern" (1994, esp. 24–27).

To be sure, at times the Jamaa's refusal to engage in free exchange may have expressed dogmatic intransigence, except that dogma was rarely a subject of debate. At issue in all these encounters was, I am tempted to say, affirmation of existence, the power of self-assertion in situations where discourses faced each other. Boundaries became fronts in a struggle for power that arose independently of subjective motives or intentions. This needs to be stated bluntly in order to make the point. It should not give the impression that Jamaa members were caught at all times in a sort of total identification with the movement that could only be qualified as neurotic. Occasional breakdown of boundaries occurred, from the point of view of genre rules, and in later years there was evidence for changes in the system itself. Without invalidating what I have said about the strictures of genre, these changes tended to confirm that the "system" was a process.

Boundaries also marked the system of memory that found expression in Shaba genre painting. As far as I am aware, they never affected talk about painting and paintings (at least not specifically; there are always *some* cultural, social, and political barriers to communication). Sharing the narratives and images of *ukumbusho* required neither initiation nor membership; all one needed to do to participate was buy a painting or two that met the requirement of being a reminder of certain widely shared experiences and memories. Other than the Jamaa movement, which for lack of distinctive, visible signs of membership would have been imperceptible to observation without communication, *ukumbusho* was expressed in striking objects that seem to come as close as anything does to social facts that can be treated *comme des choses,* data there for the picking. However, this was not how it worked in practice. Leaving aside for a moment the meaning of these images, one had to cross boundaries to become aware of the physical presence of these objects. Although some of the Shaba pictures looked very much like the kind of "airport art" that is peddled to tourists and occasional visitors to the Third World, that was not the specific form of commodification that made possible the emergence of this particular expression of popular culture. The vast production and consumption of paintings that were eventually discovered had been confined to the townships into which tourists almost never ventured, and anthropologists rarely. Occasionally, yet never conspicuously, paintings were displayed in African markets or roadside exhibitions; most transactions between painters and their customers took place face-to-face, though some of the more successful artists might occasionally employ "salesmen," usually adolescent boys. At any rate an outsider, in order to realize what these paintings represented, had to cross thresholds, physically by entering the living rooms of private homes, or mentally and socially by approaching popular painters with meaningful questions about their work.

Furthermore, genre painting was not the only kind of African painting that could be found in Shaba (and elsewhere in Zaire). That too raised questions of boundaries. In the late forties a workshop-academy had been set up in Elisabethville, later Lubumbashi, by a certain Pierre Romain-Desfossés, a French painter.[16] Convinced he had discovered certain principles of an African aesthetic, he taught young Africans to produce African art for sale to foreigners (mainly painting, some sculpture, textile prints, and ceramics). The painters of this school were encouraged to develop distinctive techniques and to produce stylized, decorative, mildly abstract works, most often depicting animals and vegetation without manifest narrative content. Realistic or figurative representation was discouraged as un-African. Christian religious motifs were encouraged because there were customers for them, but (recognizable) references to politics and history were absent. These observations are based on what I read, here and there, and heard about the orientation of that school in conversations in Lubumbashi with Pilipili and Mwenze

Kibwanga, both alumni of the Desfossés workshop. No comprehensive study exists, but I am sure it would cause us to handle the opposition between academic and popular painting in Shaba more subtly. Reproductions of early works by Desfossés students show that they did incorporate elements of style and context that are characteristic of genre painting; all of them, including the most stylized pictures produced later by Pilipili and Mwenze, represented narratives of struggle, often of violent conflict, beneath a veneer of vivid colors and striking forms. These, I hypothesize, were disguised representations of power and resistance—disguised for the foreign viewer. Going as far as was possible under conditions of direct colonial control, they were quite close to postcolonial popular "reminders" of colonial history.[17] A major difference, of course, was in the form of commodification; Desfossés- school paintings were destined exclusively for the expatriate market.

Desfossés died in 1954. By that time, several of his students had attained local and international fame; two of them (Pilipili and Mwenze) where still prolific in the mid-seventies. Also active at that time were graduates (and dropouts) from colonial art academies, among them the extraordinary Mode Muntu and the commercially successful Barnabé Chenge in Lubumbashi, who sold their work to foreign residents and, in the case of the latter, to the new Zairian middle and upper classes. I should also mention an unknown number of painters, many of whom had some exposure to art teaching, especially in missionary schools. There were some who, without direct contact with the Desfossés group, adopted its style (such as Kanyemba Yav). Others specialized in quasi-academic African landscapes (bush fires being a popular motif) and exotic velours. These were destined for the souvenir market, such as it existed, especially among lower-echelon European employees and occasional travelers; tourism never was important in industrial Shaba.

The existence of a sizable corpus of African painting inspired by colonial art schools raises the question of its relation to my subject, popular culture.[18] A remarkable result of research in the seventies, based on conversations with artists and their clients as well as on observations of the use and destination of the pictures, was the discovery of pronounced boundaries between genre painting and other practices. Many genre painters and most of their clients were only vaguely aware of the work of painters who produced for the expatriate market. When they were confronted with examples, their reaction was invariably polite but firm: "people" did not appreciate this sort of painting because it did not tell a story. These Africans had no use for "typically African" decorativeness. Their reactions expressed aesthetic judgments to the extent that they made statements about what pleased them and what didn't. The remarkable consistency and conviction with which they were proffered, however, point to ideological and, indeed, political boundaries between genre painting, as part of popular culture, and other kinds of local painting promoted by a colonial cultural and educational establishment. One need not romanticize popular painting to realize that it was a form of resistance to colonial symbolic power and an assertion of postcolonial independence. The point, however, is that the narratives and images achieved their pragmatic rather than just symbolic significance by mobilizing *ukumbusho* through generic differentiation.

Are the similarities I have noted between Jamaa discourse and popular painting to be taken as analogies (comparable structures in comparable domains, produced by comparable processes), or can they be regarded as homologous in the sense that structures, domains, and processes are actually connected as expressions we designate as popular culture? I think there are arguments for homology. The strongest may be one that leads us back to the central issue of this chapter: genre and power. Both the Jamaa movement and popular painting are based on discourses, and entail practices, of resistance to regimes of power—missionary, economic, and political—that imposed themselves on the working population of Shaba from the outside. Such resistance included critical analysis and alternative projects: in the Jamaa, a rejection of hierarchical ecclesiastic organization, perceived as reproducing colonial divisions, and a utopian dream of union in love; in genre painting, contestation of received truth about colonization and an alternative historiography. Colonial and postcolonial domination as such do not explain the particular form resistance took, but neither would resistance have been mobilized except through the specific, differentiated contents and forms that we and, I may say with some confidence, the people concerned distinguished as domains and genres of one interconnected practice: popular culture.

Power and Genre Negated

We should be wary of "things falling into place" when we analyze expressions of popular culture. It cannot be the aim of popular culture studies to reproduce, albeit on a lower social level, the positive, integrationist (or holistic) interpretations that the concept of culture *tout court* was designed to produce. Nor, important as it may be to destroy the myths of unopposed imperialism and colonialism, is demonstrating vigorous forms of cultural and political resistance the end of the story. There is more to struggle with power than struggle for power.

I assume that—after Hegel, Marx, Nietzsche, and Foucault—many would agree that power itself, much like culture, cannot be thought of as unequivocally positive (or even as neutral); wherever power is at work it negates and is negated. How does negation work with genre, which so far I have presented as a concept and practice that current parlance designates as "enabling" or "empowering" people who otherwise would remain powerless? It is tempting for anthropologists—literary scholars may be less gullible—to think of processes of generic differentiation as unequivocally creative, liberating, or at least assertive. Add to this an equally tempting populist equation between communicative processes, collective action, and emancipation, and it becomes very difficult indeed to think negatively about genres in popular culture.[19] But why should we who are engaged in blasting traditional genres of anthropological discourse—a stance we perceive as a matter of necessity if our field is to survive and as a matter of freedom that makes our critical labors worthwhile—why should we assume or expect that the creators of popular culture (producers as well as consumers) are at peace with genre (that is, with the general injunction that expressions have to come in recognized kinds) or with genres in the plural (that is, with the specific distinctions that are made)? This sort of expectation may be explained, but is not excused, if we realize it is linked to notions of quasi-neurotic repetitiveness, predictability, and cyclical orientation that belong to the image of primitive culture but also distinguish truly creative high culture from re-creative folk or popular culture.

Both the Jamaa movement and popular painting provided evidence for negative experiences with genre. In the course of ethnographic work (which was naturally positive because directed toward finding what there was and working out what could be asserted and generalized), I came upon reflections and expressions that defied generic rules and constraints by rejecting standard interpretations or by casting doubt on the entire discourse. Neither the issues raised nor those who raised them were such that these negations could be written off as a margin of deviance in an otherwise undisturbed system. In the Jamaa, there were signs of what I then called the terror of texts. There was an awareness that the discourse that drew its strength from generic formulations and practices could become a dangerous power, turning against its own inventors. To be sure, such "moments of truth" were rare.[20] And even when these moments came, they did not bring about complete liberation from rules and constraints that preoccupied the followers of the movement. Most often they raised the question of how far the Jamaa could go, under pressure from ecclesiastical authorities and competing movements, in abandoning or changing portions of doctrine and ritual practices and still survive as Jamaa—which, remember, also demanded participation in the ritual of the church. In all such decisions, genre was at the center because genre was central to defining the identity and integrity of the movement. When the mission hierarchy decided to assert its power by force—mainly but not only spiritual—the Jamaa met this unified attack with different kinds of responses, ranging from formal submission to formal schism. In either case the new situation was defined in relation to the generic rules and practices that had originally constituted the movement. Some leaders came to an arrangement with the church by agreeing to a purification of teachings considered heretical and by adopting a spiritual—nonliteral—interpretation of genres by separating them from ritual practices of gradual initiation. Others simply went underground, stuck to the original practices, and went on to attend church services and practice the rituals (such as baptism, communion, marriage, and burial). Yet others sought public recognition as a church under Zairian law and replaced Catholic rituals (including the Mass) with versions of their own (see Fabian 1994 on the Jamaa's survival through diversification). The point made by the movement's history during the past twenty years is that resistance to power is a mode of surviving not only domination from the outside, but also power within, whose accumulation may become dangerous to those it initially empowered.

Like other interpreters, I took the Jamaa to be an instance of a religious revival, an attempt to change the mission church from within. Though local schisms and excommunication had already occurred in the sixties, it took almost thirty years from the founding of the movement before it came to the definitive break initiated by the episcopal conference of 1973. Today we can have a different view on the movement's appeal among the working population, its penchant for contesting hierarchical authority, its recourse to dissimulation and subterfuge in many local confrontations with the missions and secular authorities, and the significance of the urban African content and context of its teachings. All these traits (and others that would need to be worked out, especially certain tenets of the doctrine) qualify the Jamaa as one among other expressions of Zairian popular culture. This interpretation was confirmed, for instance, by reports I received during my most recent direct contacts with the movement (in 1986 and 1987). I was told repeatedly that the so-called *katete,* the heterodox branch that seemed to have coexisted with the loyal Jamaa since its beginning (Fabian 1970, index under *katete*), was a clandestine form of the banned Kitawala, the African adaptation of the Watch Tower movement. As evidence it was claimed, among other things, that leaders and members of *katete* who had returned to their home region in the Kasai had resurfaced there as Kitawala. Be that as it may, the Kitawala itself certainly must be considered a major contributor to the emergence of a popular culture of resistance in Shaba (and beyond) since the 1920s.[21]

What about negation and genre in Shaba genre painting? I have already said that appreciation of figurative painting representing themes of shared memory often went together with the rejection of styles and subjects propagated by art schools. It would be too simple, however, to interpret this primarily, or merely, as a class-bound aesthetic choice. Urban Africans valued genre pictures not because they were the genre of people who liked genre pictures, but because the images expressed and evoked memories and made statements about colonial history and present predicaments. More than representing history (which they did in a very limited way, given the restricted number of genres carried by the market), they gave voice to history. As physical objects they were looked at, yet they were not objects of contemplation; their purpose was to occasion talk, to prompt stories. So far, so good, one is tempted to say; so this is another instance of popular culture creating a political space of freedom for thought and expression with the help of a generic set of public images, displayed in private homes where they evoke and maintain a widely shared historical narrative. Such a positive presentation would be several cuts above simply recording Shaba genre painting as a quaint and interesting feature in an otherwise drab and oppressive urban-industrial environment. Yet this would leave us with a gesture of popular self-affirmation without telling us much about the struggle that is involved when people set out to articulate memories, critical insights, and political demands as "history."

These struggles are not a matter of conjecture. It would be presumptuous to claim knowledge of what was thought and discussed among the thousands who, in one way or another, came in contact with Shaba genre painting. But we know from several painters, and above all from one of them, Tshibumba Kanda Matulu, just how much the same practice that enabled them to make a living as artists could be experienced as an aesthetic, intellectual, and political constraint. The rule of genre demanded that all the painters who wanted to reach this market reproduce a small repertoire of topics and images in great numbers. Many of them were forced to further limit their possibilities of expression by specializing in two or three genres for which they had found striking images that were in popular demand. Some painters were apparently quite happy with this, as long as they made a living (the prolific team of Nkulu wa Nkulu and Kapenda comes to mind); others, who had understood, perhaps more deeply than their colleagues, that the people buying their products were engaged in a search for meaning and sense in history, were frustrated because the genre market had so little tolerance for artistic originality and historical specificity.

Tshibumba, for instance, certainly was aware that controls on free expression exercised by the political regime, and the aesthetic regime that controlled the market for genre painting, could converge from the point of view of the critical painter-historian he saw himself as being. Both put limits on what he could paint; both forced him, as he himself was eager to point out, to compromise where his own visions would have been offensive or to introduce anachronistic elements (such as showing Lumumba waving Mobutu's party flag), because these pictures, after all, were painted "to be sold," that is, to be accepted as genre pictures. Tshibumba's case is ethnographically interesting because it documents his struggle with genre when he set out to paint, in his words, the "entire history of the country." He was someone who shed the burden of authorized narratives of the colonial past and enriched Shaba popular culture with one of its most striking creations, visual as well as verbal. He accomplished this as a genre painter who, to employ a culturally appropriate expression, "ate the power" of genre and derived from it the strength to carry out the critical work of resistance and contestation.

The expression "to eat power" reminds me to address at least a few brief remarks to another kind of negation of genre that (though I, like others, insist on distinguishing popular culture from folklore) seems to be widely operative in practices of incorporating customs and traditions into expressions of contemporary culture. I became aware of this in the course of an ethnography of a play conceived and performed by the Mufwankolo troupe of popular actors in Lubumbashi (see Fabian 1990b). Starting with a saying that provided the theme (*le pouvoir se mange entier,* power is eaten whole), going on with the selection of a setting, protagonists, and plot, and culminating in a message that was a critique of the current political power structure in the country, this event resulted from a process of multiple negations of genre. The saying itself looked like a traditional proverb, yet, as an unsuccessful search for its authentic form demonstrated, it derived its evocative power from the fact that it could not be put down as just another among thousands of proverbs. (As we shall see in the next chapter, no exact equivalent of the French saying could be found in a local language.) The play that was to illustrate or enact the meaning of *le pouvoir se mange entier* was construed around a village chief, his corrupt advisers, and an unruly peasantry. The actors needed to draw on symbols, personages, forms of speech, practices, and so forth (including a real village in which the final filmed performance was staged) that would ensure the mask of folksiness that could hide the play's political message. On the one hand, especially when one considered that numerous songs in local languages made up about half of the playing time, this effect was achieved by evoking genres the audience would recognize as traditional. At the same time, it is obvious that this worked in the play only because the rules that would have governed the performance of these genres in their traditional context were not respected. During the long discussions, rehearsals, and repeated changes that preceded the final performance, Mufwankolo and his actors—who are without doubt among the most widely known and appreciated creators of Shaba popular culture—showed an amazingly clear awareness of what can best be described as folkloric generalization that had to be achieved rather than simply presupposed. Looked at closely, such generalization is not a transformation of something that exists only specifically—tradition—into something that needs to be general to exist—popular culture. What is being transformed, after having been selected and confronted, is tradition whose power and authority never existed except as its ability to differentiate and define genres of communication and performance. "Eating power" is not only represented but enacted when popular culture transforms tradition.[22]

It is perhaps not surprising, then, that during the time of my intensive work with the troupe (which also included preparations for a highly controversial command performance to commemorate the first seventy-five years of Catholic missions in Shaba) I witnessed many instances of power play within and around the group of actors. The question arose of whether the piece should be submitted to the political authorities for approval, then there was a heated debate on how far one could go in keeping the plot seemingly inoffensive without compromising artistic integrity. In fact, gender and ethnic conflicts within the group at one time caused Mufwankolo to embark on a soul-searching moral *causerie*. All these issues showed another dimension of *le pouvoir se mange entier*, one that was not just being enacted or presented but that determined the creative process itself.

Thinking about genre and power in the context of popular theater in Shaba leads one to an observation that, although it cannot be pursued to any extent in these essays, should at least be noted.

In the cases of religious discourse and genre painting, emergence was described as a process of generic differentiation. Popular theater seems to pose a problem in this regard. The little we know of its history (see Fabian 1990b, 45–57) suggests that it started after World War II with the production of imported French plays (sometimes, but not always, translated into Swahili) in schools and youth movements. It seems that small groups of performers soon began to improvise their own sketches, adding music and dance and experimenting with impersonation and parody, often inspired by records and movies.[23] The differentiation that then took place, however, was apparently between comedy, music, and theater (no doubt conditioned by the fact that music became a mass medium when the beginnings of a recording industry were established in the late forties; theater troupes like Mufwankolo's had to wait for the seventies before they appeared regularly on local television). Within popular theater itself, development moved toward comedy or farce as the dominant form. But then, this was perhaps inevitable. No other form is as well suited to criticizing and contesting power from a position of relative powerlessness. In the seventies, historical drama and folkloric dance theater were performed by university students and groups led by expatriates; these genres were not the stuff Mufwankolo needed, as he would have put it, to add salt to the lives of the ordinary people who were his avid spectators and commentators.

A Lesson to Be Learned

The purpose of this chapter has been to show that a concept like genre can help us better understand the role popular culture may play in situations where power meets resistance. Shaba popular culture demonstrated its capacity to create spaces of freedom for expression in movements (among others) such as the Jamaa, genre painting, and theater. Such accomplishments rest not on single acts of contestation but rather on repetitive enactment of ideas, on practices that are socially constituted. The issue of power and resistance in studies of popular culture therefore cannot be reduced to determining whether or not, or when and where, expressions of popular culture qualify as acts of resistance; what we need to understand is how popular culture creates power to resist power. The situations and examples we have examined suggest that popular culture owes its precarious existence to practices that must each face the problem of power from within.[24] Which is another way of saying that what we are likely to find when we closely examine the working of popular culture are processes of the same kind as those that oppose popular culture to various forms of domination.

In critical studies of power and culture we expose oppression and record resistance; when we take sides with the survivors, it is essential to realize that there is more to survival than blocking aggression or subverting domination, both of which popular culture seems to be capable of. Survival is *staying* alive, and that has something to do with the capacity to establish domains of expression through generic differentiation without allowing genre to take on the kind of power that would make it impossible to remain creative. And survival also entails the capacity to carry on with, to use Roy Wagner's insightful phrase, the invention of culture.

When we raise the issue of power in critiques of anthropology and other kinds of dominant Western discourse, we inevitably envisage *us* facing *them*. This undoubtedly is a first prerequisite for gaining a critical perspective. But we miss the point of our own findings about power and resistance in popular culture as long as we fail to realize that a struggle with power that may look like theirs, because it seems to occur on the other side of a dividing line between the West and the rest, is equally ours. It is just an instance of the kind of resistance and liberation that makes it possible in the first place to perceive resistance to power as an intellectual task.

3

Time and Movement in Popular Culture

Genre, I have argued, allows us to conceptualize the process that produces, through differentiation of forms, a particular domain of popular culture and to locate sites where struggle with and for power takes place. Nevertheless, in its common understanding, genre remains a concept so much associated with classifying that it is easy to forget its kinship with generating. It is now time to face a danger inherent in any interpretation of culture that deploys concepts of form quasi-mechanically and uncritically. That danger lies in exaggerated presentations of culture amounting to caricature. In presenting ethnography in terms of forms (traits, patterns, configurations, structures, networks, webs of significance, and so forth), we must also pay attention to movement, and therefore to time, not just as an ad libitum extension of inquiry into history, but as a way of doing justice to essential aspects of what constitutes the object of inquiry. That goes for anthropology, the study of culture(s) in general, even though during the history of our discipline we have often neglected that rule (as I tried to show in *Time and the Other*). The special significance, and effect, of studying popular culture seems to have been, at least in my own work, to sensitize anthropology to time and movement in the constitution of its objects. Let me try to unpack this observation as best I can by removing several layers of theoretical obfuscation.

Dominant Space and Resistant Time

One of the foremost obstacles to understanding popular culture has been the tendency in culture theory to privilege space over time. In older versions, practices counted as (parts of) culture only if they could be assigned to distinctive geographic areas; what time had done to, or with, a culture could not be considered unless that culture had managed to occupy a space. A methodological corollary of such a theory was that culture—never mind how much its inner, organic, or ideal unity was celebrated—was thought of as a combination of parts. A static record, the spatial distribution of elements, called culture traits, could then be translated into history; spatially bounded culture areas could be understood as traditions.

True, by the time they encountered African urban life British functionalists and American culturalists had moved away from the tenets of evolutionism and diffusionism. The urge to tie culture to physical space gave way to fascination with imagined analytical spaces that were called social or cultural systems. Still, as we saw, these modern anthropologists had great difficulty perceiving cultural practices that did not occupy bounded territories as anything but symptoms of displacement and confusion. Eventually, concerns with the effects of migration and the consequences of culture clash were channeled into studies of acculturation and change. "Change" is a term that suggests temporality (*tempora mutantur,* the times they are a-changin'), but unlike its predecessors, evolution and diffusion, it no longer stood for movement (on a scale or through a region). Conceptually, change was tied to identity, and there can be little doubt that, in studies of change, the cards were usually stacked in favor of identity (by assuming that change disturbed identity or, when it could no longer be avoided, always moved toward a new identity). On the whole, loss of identity was much more talked about than its creation. Moreover, for sociologists and anthropologists, interest in change more often than not expressed concerns for permanence and stability that go together with privileging space over time in conceptions of culture.

A way of developing a more specific argument from these general allegations may be to consider that the emergence of African urban culture was also conceptualized with the help of such apparently temporal notions as modernization. We should therefore take a closer look at the ways opposition between tradition and modernity in culture can be conceived as a time relation.

Tradition, especially the phrase "traditional culture"—once a concept that did not have to be justified in anthropological discourse—had come under attack at just about the time I was trying to piece together the sources of Jamaa teaching. The founder himself had been an ethnographer of Luba culture (and had published several scholarly papers) before he thought of adapting Christianity to Bantu thought. When he eventually presented the results of his efforts (notably in his *Catéchèse bantoue* [Tempels 1948]) and began to assemble a group of followers, he often referred to traditional customs as examples or outright models for the doctrine and practices that were to become the Jamaa movement. When I later attempted to retrace this process (which was not easy, because Tempels had become cautious in his writings and his strongest appeals to African tradition were made in his oral teaching), I always insisted that Jamaa doctrine was a true synthesis rather than a syncretist mélange. I tried to show this in specific instances, such as the incorporation of animal fables and other obviously African stories into Jamaa teaching (Fabian 1977). Nevertheless I still imagined that, on the whole, this *new* form of religious enthusiasm faced *old* forms of culture that might as well be called traditional.

I must have been aware then of anthropological critiques of the concept; if not, I became so soon after. Arguments were directed mainly against false reifications of tradition (through idealization, generalization, or simplification). Abandoning such reification implied, or should have implied, that tradition was no longer to be treated as an entity, elements of which could be selected to become ingredients of modern orientations. Another point of attack for revisions should have been the alleged ahistoricity, in fact timelessness, of tradition. But somehow this aspect seemed to be taken care of by African history, which was just then emerging as a vigorous new field. As yet, we were not quite prepared to consider that the issue of reification is not really being addressed when one concept, African tradition, is recognized as reified and replaced by another, African history, just because the latter is new, still being formulated, and used in convincing arguments for abolishing the old term. Only by the late sixties did we realize that such problems were matters of epistemology, not just of the technical refinement of our scientific vocabulary. More was needed than to denounce reification, namely an understanding of, one might say, the specific procedure that was used to put tradition in its place in schemes of interpreting culture.

Today I would argue that, at least in anthropology, a classical allochronistic strategy was operating when modernity and tradition were distinguished. On some ultimate, cosmological level, difference was stated in terms of distance in time. Tradition essentially belonged to the past; it came before modernity. Even if it was conceived dynamically, it was always not yet what it was to become through modernization. And this amounted to denial of coevalness, a refusal to think of tradition and modernity as contemporary. On reflection, it is clear that the two could not relate to each other—more precisely, urban Africans could not have related to (adopted, adapted, mixed, preserved, rejected, revived) tradition—except insofar as tradition was copresent with modernity.[1] In the interpretation of culture, archaeological metaphors such as strata and sequences may serve structural analyses (as reconstruction); they are misleading when they are supposed to describe cultural practices such as remembering the past that are central to popular culture. Popular (collective) memory, whose task I take to be the production of the present (Fabian 1996), does not work like archaeology (though, come to think of it, much of archaeology may work like popular memory).

Acknowledging the copresence of modernity and tradition does not mean the relation is atemporal. Involving essentially interaction, rather than the mere impact of one on the other, copresence results in transformations, hence in process. Furthermore, such a process must logically be a practice that belongs to (or is controlled by) neither tradition nor modernity. For something other than sheer obliteration to happen, people cannot be imagined to be tied down by tradition or swept away by modernity. The study of popular culture, to return to my topic, can be said to have made us rediscover freedom as a condition of survival through creativity in situations that, through the lens of culture theory, could only be viewed as too precarious to sustain anything but imitations, resemblances, or caricatures of culture. In the revisions that are needed, therefore, culture theory is bound to lose a certain grandeur. At one time culture, any culture, could be envisioned as an artful, well-constructed edifice; diversity could be celebrated because we thought of culture in terms of spaces coexisting in a universe essentially, though not incidentally, free of domination and strife. In popular culture we have a concept and discourse capable of perceiving (apart from the vital, vigorous, and creative) the unforeseen, transient, and precarious—the essentially temporal and therefore temporary aspects of cultural processes.

These reflections on space over time took off from what could be termed old spatializations of culture. But there are also new, or newer, ways to privilege space over time. Among them are two current theoretical trends, ethnicity and globalization, that may conflict with the approach to popular culture I have been advocating.

Though the concept itself is not necessarily, not even obviously, spatial, the theory of ethnicity in Africa owes its present prominence to the critique of territorial concepts, such as anthropology's long-honored unit of study and comparison, the tribe. At first glance it seems there is much convergence in thought about popular culture and ethnicity. By the late sixties it was clear that most forms of ethnicity, certainly those that posed social and political problems and became the target of funded research, were invented (no pejorative sense intended) by groups of displaced people *after* they had migrated or for other reasons lost their place in their societies owing to wars, the collapse of nation-states, or the demise of colonial regimes. Ethnics are people, we were told, to whom separation from their territory of origin and their past has become a problem of identity in relating to their new surroundings. As an assemblage of cultural symbols and practices that ethnics brought along, remembered, and more often than not (re)invented, ethnicity could be construed for the purpose of organizing action such as claiming civil rights, access to jobs, economic resources, and political power. Paradoxically, though somehow tied to displacement, to separation of place from identity, ethnicity could also become a desirable, or inescapable, idiom of cultural, social, and political practices for populations that had remained in place and had never thought of their habits of speech, dress, or cooking as "ethnic." As it turned out, it did not take long for invented ethnicity to become commoditized in a vast array of goods for consumption, from food and fabric patterns to music and therapeutic rituals.

It cannot be denied that, in the situations that produced African popular culture, elements appeared in the past and continue to exist in the present that seem to fit what has been conceptualized as ethnicity. But closer examination reveals that African "tribalism" (to use a term that has more currency among those concerned than "ethnicity") has been different in its origins as well as in its later development. One way to probe these differences is to ask in what sense theories of ethnicity can be counted among conceptualizations that privilege space over time. In Zaire many, if not most, of the ethnic identities (symbolized, for instance, by a label supposedly marking common descent, or by languages purported to be distinctive of a group) were demonstrably colonial impositions, administrative and missionary. The overriding concern of colonial regimes was to define colonial space and to map territorial divisions on various levels down to localities (Noyes 1992). How arbitrary these impositions were can be seen from the fact that they were easily ignored when the colony faced the problem of securing its external frontiers. When these were set, most of them cut through linguistic and cultural areas; when cultural specificity could not be assigned a territory, it was ignored.

Although most colonial ethnic identifications remained extraneous impositions, respected only under constraint, some were accepted by the population, though always interpreted and transformed in the course of history. For more and more Zairian cases we are beginning to get critical histories.[2] Of course, that these identities were imposed, and in that sense also invented, does not mean they were and are not real; they had lasting and sometimes bloody consequences. We should just keep in mind that neither when it is adopted as an ideology nor when it is used as an explanatory concept can ethnicity be passed off as given or necessary, and certainly not as a typical response to modernity.

In the postindependence struggles for political power (which in Zaire pitted proponents of a unitary state against federalists and separatists), ethnic strife was often taken as evidence for a relapse into traditional tribal wars, whereas it was to a large extent a colonial heritage. Today, thirty years later, the moribund country seems ready to embark again on tribal wars along ethnic lines (see the recent clashes between "Katangese" and "Kasaians" and the ethnic cleansings that took their victims among the latter). Undoubtedly what happened, and what is still to come, will be put down to atavism, whereas it is clearly part of a global trend expressive of the failure of the nation-state that had once been an instrument of colonization and continues to be the preferred form of political control in the capitalist system of domination over Third World countries.

Although I could not refrain from stating my position in this forceful manner, I do not pretend to have a clear understanding of the events we are witnessing in Africa and, on daily television, closer to home. Among the people in Shaba whom I had gotten to know as united in creating popular religion and art, who shared a common language and remembered a common history, many took sides, voluntarily or not, in the ethnic war. This leaves me sad and depressed but all the more convinced that there is more to popular culture than the expression of ethnicity. Based on what I learned through the years, I can say with confidence that, although regional cultural differences exist and ethnic differences frequently are a topic (especially in comments on politics), the creations of Zairian popular culture cannot be said either simply to reflect cultural reinvention of ethnic identity or to have their main function as vehicles for asserting ethnic identity. Many may feel that the present tense is inappropriate in my statement (and there is a problem, if only because the "ethnographic present" is problematic whenever we employ it); but until we have incontestable evidence to the contrary, we can assume that the production of a common popular culture continues, perhaps in forms we are as yet unable to discern.

Take, for example, Zairian popular music, whose creative center at this moment is no longer in Kinshasa but in Paris, Brussels, London, and other places where exiled Zairians congregate. The ethnic origins of famous creators and performers are well known; yet none of them could have gained his or her prominence within one ethnic group. The economics of popular music alone, the market for its commodified products, and the patterns of consumption preclude ethnicity's becoming a determinant of this form of popular culture. This is perhaps most clearly visible linguistically. Almost all composers and performers participated in a development that has moved toward an increasing dominance of Lingala. This language has been associated with the national capital, with national institutions such as the army, perhaps also with the regime's party and bureaucracy, but above all with "modern life" and urbanity, even by those who do not "use" Lingala except when they listen to records or the radio.[3] When, at least occasionally, certain star performers chose lyrics in one of the other national languages (Kikongo, Tshiluba, and Swahili), perhaps even in one or another "tribal" language, they celebrated diversity, not ethnic identity.

Similarly, many among the countless religious movements and new churches have a pronounced regional orientation, but not even Kimbangism, recognized by everyone as originally Kongo (that is, coming from the Kongo ethnic region in lower Zaire where the prophet Simon Kimbangu was active until his arrest in 1921) and often associated with regional politics in the past, can unequivocally be said to promote Kongo ethnicity, which is of little concern to its many followers in other regions of the country. The church itself has a national and even international orientation (Martin 1975; Asch 1983).

Recent assertions to the contrary notwithstanding, I saw in the seventies no evidence for ethnicity in popular painting.[4] In Shaba the shared regime of memory, expressed in the accepted canon of genres, did not exclude regional and in this sense "ethnic" specificity; after all, colonial and postcolonial experiences were made in specific places and situations. However, genre painters and their customers were of diverse ethnic origins. When an exceptional artist such as Tshibumba Kanda Matulu broke away from genre painting and defined himself as a historian, he went to great lengths to stress national unity, if only because he needed the nation as the subject of a history whose narrative he could oppose to colonial and academic accounts. In this respect Tshibumba emulated his hero Patrice Lumumba, who pursued his resolutely unitarian course because he knew this was the only way to establish his country as a political power vis-à-vis the former colonizer and on the international scene. Even earlier popular histories, such as the *Vocabulary of the Town of Elisabethville,* maintained a regional, rather than an ethnic, orientation within a larger colonial frame (more about Tshibumba and this document later in this chapter).

As I argued in the preceding chapter, work on popular theater in Shaba showed that its creators and performers consciously avoided ethnic identification. When they evoked ethnic specificity (in names, rituals, institutions, songs and stories, or even in certain stock characters in their plays), they did so to create a generalized idiom, a "folksy" style that goes with the predominantly comic genre of their performances.

Finally, to return to my first project of research, Jamaa doctrine understood itself as transcending *bukabila* (tribalism, ethnicity). Some observers have pointed out that the movement's membership was predominantly "Kasaian." If that was so—there are no demographic statistics to prove this—it would reflect a profile created by preferential hiring policies implemented by the mining and railway companies. In that case—assuming the ethnic identity of Jamaa members was predominantly Kasaian (as defined by the companies)—it would be all the more remarkable that the movement resolutely rejected ethnic bias, for instance, in its recruitment practices. Jamaa groups that seemed to stress ethnic ties (I can think of only one, but I heard allegations about others) were regarded as suspicious if not deviant.

In sum, among the domains of popular culture I encountered in my work, none was claimed, or could be identified, as an "ethnic" cultural property. Such a conclusion, even if accepted, may not settle the issue. The question remains to what extent a focus on popular culture may lead one to overlook ethnicity—perhaps as a misguided effort to save a militantly populist concept of cultural identity. With his usual perspicacity and command of ethnography, Wim van Binsbergen recently seemed to argue that ethnicity covers more of what others try to catch with the concept of popular culture (and does it better). He rejects popular culture because he thinks anthropology would not need to employ a term that actually signals the effect of hegemonic, oppressive forces if it were not itself affected by these forces:

> The "popular culture" of African peasants and urban poor today is hardly considered, by its academic analysts, to be the mold out of which a national culture will spring, its increasingly articulate genius expressed in literary and musical products worthy to be enshrined among the universal heritage of mankind. Popular culture as a term has come to reflect a reality of subordination, incorporation, hegemony and globalization which has affected the cultural producers in Africa *just as it has affected anthropology itself.* (1995, 33)

This "academic analyst" begs to differ, and he is not the only one whose work affirms what it is here said to deny. As I did in the first chapter, van Binsbergen senses a connection between anthropology and popular culture that he also describes as one of homology, that is, as arising from the same processes. Whereas I take this to be a sign of strength, a prospect of understanding based on affinity, he counts that affinity as a weakness, one that I assume he sees as endangering anthropology's scientific status. This does not mean he advocates sticking to paradigms that have outlived their usefulness. He knows we need alternative concepts now that we have lost faith in both culture and the tribe as units of study. I am not convinced, however, that he is right when he links this loss of faith to a loss of a "monopoly on knowledge production concerning exotic societies" (that monopoly was an illusion; all that was lost was an illusion) and then blames this loss of status on anthropology's prostituting itself (my term, his meaning) to other sciences in "development intervention or aid." (He might also have mentioned such respectable academic disciplines as philosophy, history, literary criticism, and whatever is encompassed in "cultural studies.") I am not at all prepared to follow him (Why would I toil at these essays?) when he concludes that it "is largely in this frame that I understand anthropology's recent adoption of a term like 'popular culture,' which has no systematic status in the discipline and would turn out to be rather dubious if subjected to theoretical anthropological analysis" (1995, 33).

Of course popular culture has no "systematic status"; we needed the concept because we realized that systematic culture theory had failed us. It would be strange indeed if popular culture theory that was formulated to challenge classical anthropological culture theory would have to legitimize itself by the standards of the latter. But van Binsbergen is less certain about his rejection of popular culture than he sounds. It does him credit when, in the concluding paragraphs of the paper, he first reluctantly admits that the concept could very well apply "as a symbolic celebration of globalization" (about which more presently) and then ends with a statement I cannot refrain from quoting at length (notice that it is no longer really addressed to the concept of popular culture but is directed to a kind of reality he cannot help but acknowledge):

> Does popular culture in Africa do nothing but reinforce and express the state of encapsulation and reduced symbolic competence of peasants and urban poor . . . ? Much to our surprise . . . (and in a way that leaves hope both for anthropology and for its habitual research subjects), the answer must be "no." For in popular culture, if nowhere else, the underdog strikes back: culture is not totally dependent and borrowed—on the contrary, it can be seen by the actors, even when bricolaged, as very much one's own (just like language), and therefore creates an issue for mediating with the outside world. It may build new expressive boundaries around the local community, but not to seal this off from the outside world, but to negotiate with it. (1995, 34)

I could not agree more. As to playing ethnicity against popular culture, I suspect the positions that are taken in this debate are, in the end, political ones: unitarian-universalist versus pluralist-relativist. The only wedge I can drive into this is to ask which concept has a better chance of overcoming space-over-time thinking—assuming that the perniciousness of the latter is worth worrying about.

Globalization is another idea that needs to be addressed in these essays. Even more obviously than ethnicity, it is originally a spatial concept, albeit one that seems to dissolve two notions essential to any orientation that privileges space over time: locality (place) and territory (boundaries). At first glance it is tempting to think of popular culture as a product of globalization, if only because, as I have argued, it is not a local or regional phenomenon. Fashions of dress, styles of music and dance, religious discourses, and visual creations that are produced in contemporary Africa may be consumed anywhere in the world. Still, I hesitate to approach African popular culture from a globalist perspective. The problem I have is a suspicion: globalization theory may not be all that different from, say, classical theories of cultural evolution. It may encourage what I called elsewhere space-time fusions, between here and now and there and then (Fabian 1991b, 229–30). After all, globalization is diagnosed, and formulated as a discourse, in central places; a global epistemic position is difficult to imagine: Who can speak from "nowhere in particular"? Like its predecessor or cousin, world-system theory, globalization theory has room for centers and peripheries (the global is more global in some places than in others). It is easy to see that this can only result in assigning to African popular culture a place on a scale of globalization earlier, lower, or less complete than that occupied by the creations of "developed" countries. And that would be just another way of denying presence to African popular culture.

But there could be a different way of thinking about globalization that may take off from spatial categories but ends with a position that does not involve privileging space over time. Let me begin this argument with a commonsense observation. Literally, "global" means something like pertaining to the earth as a whole. Although this is a familiar notion that was entertained by romantic thinkers such as Herder, this is not really what we mean when we talk about globalization as a process. The actual extension or spread of objects, practices, or organizations to the point where they can be called worldwide cannot be qualified ipso facto as global. By the sixteenth century the Catholic Church had a worldwide presence. Was it therefore a global institution? When we use the term now, we are trying to catch radical changes in our relation to goods, institutions, and practices that emerge when boundaries (territorial, social, political) that gave specificity—local meaning—to life are stretched to the point where they no longer produce specificity.

If pressed, I would characterize my view of globalization as dialectical. Thinking dialectically always requires both attention to specifics and a notion of totality. In contrast to, say, classificatory or typological approaches, which also work with the general and the specific, dialectics holds that the relation between specifics and totalities is, first, not abstract-logical but concrete-historical and second, not necessarily peaceful, rational, or predictable. Applying this kind of reasoning to African popular culture generally, we come to the following conclusions. Local expressions are neither representations nor cases of global popular culture. The local *is* the global under the conditions of globalization that obtain at this moment in history. Globalization is not a factual state of affairs; it is a process ridden with conflict and contradictions, and that, once again, is one of the reasons an integrative, systemic concept of culture *tout court* is no longer sufficient.

Be that as it may, these musings about a dialectical approach to globalization take us back to a key problem in the study of popular culture that I raised earlier: how to take seriously, theoretically and practically, its presence and contemporaneity. Let me now make a new start in addressing that question.

Time Respected: Present and Presence

On trips between towns in Shaba and during an occasional tour upcountry, I drove through villages. I saw the smoke of cookstoves rising against the dawn, the silhouettes of people outlined against a fire at night. Sometimes I stopped for a chat or to buy a basket of mushrooms from a market woman shriveled by hard work and age, who counted greasy banknotes and urged me to spend more. I saw men smoking clay pipes confer in the shade of a communal hut and watched women pound grain while their children played on the clean-swept red laterite ground. I recall the smell of villages, an aroma of smoke and fermented manioc that was noticeable perhaps a mile away. I met work parties on their way home, shouldering their hoes and machetes; I admired the elegance of fishermen standing up in dugout canoes to cast their nets or aim their spears. Now and then I saw groups of people, half naked and covered with dirt, congregating to mourn a death; or I glimpsed others, their faces smeared with white clay, as they celebrated overcoming some crisis, perhaps the birth of twins. When I had visitors with me, I would point out little hutlike structures: "Shrines to the ancestors," I would comment knowledgeably. Often I noticed odd objects placed in the fork of a dead tree or pieces of white cloth tied around branches, tokens of acknowledgment of another world of ghosts and ancestral spirits. And there was the day when I stopped at a roadside stand and told the two market women, whom I recognized as Lunda, that Mwant Yav, their ruler, had just died. At once they began wailing and showing their grief with appropriate gestures of distress. They uttered lamentations that I am sure conformed to age-old Lunda etiquette. I remember how touched I was, and how I caught a whiff of the glory of a ruler whose death could make market women weep. When one of them, addressing me and her companion, blamed death on the breach of a tabu—on his travels, Mwant Yav had crossed a river no ruling chief should cross—I felt I had been taken into their confidence.

On all these occasions, I *read* African culture. I decoded signs, a skill, however limited and haphazardly assembled, I had acquired from years of ethnographic reading and from occasional instruction by missionary ethnographers and African friends. I never collected firsthand, in-depth knowledge of traditions that were alive in the villages that dotted the vast stretches of savanna between the mining towns. I cannot claim authority as an ethnographer of African culture based on prolonged fieldwork consecrated by deprivation, danger, and suffering from ill health and lack of comfort. Not that this African life did not touch me; on the contrary, it inspired in me a kind of paralyzing respect for the daunting requirements an ethnographer would have to meet, such as mastering a tonal language, which I felt were beyond me. Though it was omnipresent in the region where I carried out my research, African culture—as studied, imagined, and proclaimed by anthropologists—did not become present to me except in those moments I tried to evoke with my random list of recollections. To do "classic" ethnography, I must have felt (but was certainly not able to put into words at the time), would never amount to more than adding to, improving, perhaps correcting texts that others had already written. I was wrong about this—no culture is understood simply because it has been conveyed to an archive by means of writing and thereby placed in the past time of tradition. In my confused search for a theoretical position that would free me from the obligation to reproduce what is as it was before modern colonization, I had, like many anthropologists of my generation, decided to investigate change—that is, culture in the present. Little did I know then that my training in two paradigms that were considered the most old-fashioned (diffusionism) and the most modern (structuralism-functionalism) had left me woefully ill equipped to do anthropology "in the present."

By design and by the usual concatenation of accidents that make ethnographers select their terrain (as in *faire du terrain,* to conduct field research), I had decided on Zaire as an area. On 14 January 1966 I landed in Léopoldville, capital of the Democratic Republic of the Congo. First impressions, we know, can be ominous, though it may take a lifetime to figure out exactly what the omen meant when we recorded it. Two experiences, one visual, the other acoustic, left lasting imprints on my mind. The first one, together with an interpretation that now sounds a bit coy, became the very first entry in my personal diary (in German; at that time I still thought in my native language): "What I have seen of this town so far strikes me like the flat feet of the market women who balance loads on their heads, feet that grip the dust of the road: houses and neighborhoods are glued to the soil, almost disappearing in the low vegetation. But all of this lives and carries something that is still strange to me. The beginning has been easy for me—I still live in my old world." The other is a recollection I have often recounted but have never before put on paper. My memory places it at the end of this first day in Kinshasa, then still called Léopoldville, a day that began with a long flight from Brussels, continued with a long trip from the airport to the town, and ended at the place where I was to stay for a few days before I continued toward Katanga-Shaba. I was in bed in a room at a mission in the middle of Dendale township, trying to get some sleep. Around the square where the mission buildings lay, loudspeakers from what seemed at least four bars or dance halls blasted

Zairian music into the night air; each played a different record, yet in my tortured head they created a common effect, a kind of pulse caused by a seemingly never-ending repetition of guitar riffs. Here was African life that assaulted me physically, made its presence painfully felt. I was about to go out of my mind, as the saying goes, when a tropical downpour swept all noise from the square.

In retrospect, I am amazed at how ominous these two first-day impressions were, each in its kind and both by their contrast. It took me many years to realize that if we would really follow the ideal of observation from a distance as the only reliable source of experience—the kind that comes easy because we need not leave, mentally, our old world to observe the new (in fact we must not leave it mentally if we want to fulfill our mission as observers)—we would forever be forced to make sense of what we saw through allegory—flat feet, flat houses—by inventing interpretations or testing theories that reveal what the visible hides. Present to us in such an endeavor is our theory; absent are those on whom it is pronounced.

Not so with my first encounter with popular music. It was too direct, literally too painful, to become the object of instant reflection. Whatever made its presence felt did so on its own terms. It belonged there; I didn't. For years, I must confess, I resented Zairian popular music until I met it on its own ground. Eventually I was seduced by its power and beauty; I am still privately embarrassed that it took me so long to recognize it as perhaps Zaire's richest and most distinctive gift to the continent, and indeed the world.

But that is just one way of stating what needs to be said repeatedly in these essays: Had I chosen to "do an ethnography" of one of the recognized groups, the presence of my object of study would not have been a problem; it would have been there to be observed and recorded. That, at least, was what my vaguely scientific, vaguely positivist, training led me to expect. The transformation of noise into music—if I may attach allegorical significance to my experience after all—describes an essential aspect of my discovery of popular culture, an epistemological lesson I have since spelled out in much of my writing. It takes time to do ethnography because, for any kind of anthropology that aspires to more than filling preformulated rubrics with data and perhaps playing a preset theoretical game or two, it takes time to be in the presence of what is to be studied, and then again to come up with representations that do not have to deny that presence. It is not the theoretical gaze that makes presence—the so-called givenness of data is an illusion, as more and more practitioners of my discipline are now ready to admit—it takes action and interaction that may start (remember the noisy night in Dendale) with sensuous and mental experiences of aggression and suffering.

Lest this be misunderstood as romanticizing fieldwork in exotic places, I should say that I now take presence to be a condition of all empirical inquiry in cultural anthropology. Still, it was important to show (I will say more later) that this insight imposed itself in my own work as I faced expressions of African culture that eventually became part of something more encompassing, which I now call popular culture. Though it is obviously contingent on the historical situation and the context—the town rather than the village—this is the epistemological significance of popular culture that may be missed by critics who experience their work as a continuation of classic ethnography in traditional villages.

Time Contested: Popular History and Chronology

After reviewing, however briefly, how time perceived and conceptualized, time negated and acknowledged, informs anthropological inquiry into popular culture, we should now take a look at "ways with time" in domains of popular culture that became objects of my inquiries.

Time is a topic that seems to invite writers to take the grand view. Sweeping generalizations about African conceptions of time have been made in the past, usually with the claim that they represent traditional African thought.[5] I cannot offer similar abstractions from what I know about contemporary African culture. I used the expression "ways with time" to indicate a pragmatic approach to conceptualizations of time in domains I can claim to have studied in some depth. Pragmatic means that I consider certain approaches, such as semiotic or logical analyses of terms and grammatical elements expressing temporal relations, at best preparatory to what I am after: an understanding of how ideas of time organize discourses that in turn inform communication and interaction.

The findings to be presented now come again from a domain of popular culture, one that is best characterized as an emerging historiology: [6] the shared memories of colonial and postcolonial history objectified in written texts, oral accounts, and visual images. Because time in writing, telling, and picturing history is still a theme too vast for the purpose of this essay (and because I already discussed some aspects of my sources in the two previous chapters), I shall introduce a further limitation. I shall concentrate on one aspect of historiology, namely chronology, the sequential presentation of events by means of dating. This will allow me to address at the same time a theme that underlies all these reflections on popular culture: I shall pay special attention to differences as confrontations between popular and high-culture academic historiology and as instances of contestation and resistance.

My understanding of "chronology" is that of the educated layman. Strictly speaking, chronology is a field of knowledge about dating, a multidiscipline. When I employ the term I have in mind not so much methods and techniques as the results of chronological research: dates and lists of dates. That the sources I will be commenting on do not speak of dating in a general manner is part of the challenge they pose.

Points of Departure: Discrepancies

One of the most vexing problems the interpreter of popular historiology has to face is apparent gross errors in dating events and periods. My first example comes from Tshibumba's painted and narrated history of Zaire (see Fabian 1996). From the sources available to him (popular memory, his own recollections, a few books, newspapers, and radio reports) he composed an amazingly detailed and complex history of his country from times ancestral to the present. As a literate person, Tshibumba perfectly understood the significance of dates and chronologies. During the process of assembling his history he occasionally noticed errors and either corrected them or stated that he did not know the exact date of certain events. Sometimes he showed concern for subtle points, such as when he dated Congolese independence to both 1959, the year it was claimed by a popular uprising, and 1960, when it was granted by Belgium. He handled with aplomb the bewildering confusion of events during the two decades that followed (the tragic career of Patrice Lumumba, the Katanga secessions, the rebellions, and subsequent power struggles that academic historians are still busy sorting out). But there were moments, for instance, in his account of the establishment of colonial rule, when Tshibumba appeared to make serious mistakes in dating events.

Take the painting depicting the encounter between the Portuguese seafarer Diogo Cão and Banza Kongo, as Tshibumba calls the Kongo ruler Cão met first (fig. 2). There are numerous layers of significance in the image itself (most conspicuously, the nineteenth-century explorer's uniform Diogo Cão wears and the protagonists' turning their backs to the viewer); others are added by an inscription on the painting: "Diego Cao and the king of Kongo. 'Yes, this is the river Nzade (Zaïre),' Banza said. A few days later, there was the meeting of Stanley and Diego's group which was composed of Dhanis, Bodson, and the others." Although Tshibumba correctly identified the beginning of the colonial era with the arrival of the Portuguese at the mouth of the Congo (the first sighting was in 1482; actual encounter with Africans took place during Cão's second voyage in 1485), he seemed confused, in fact way off, when he made Henry Morton Stanley and certain Belgians who worked for King Leopold's International African Association and later the Congo

2. *Diogo Cão and the King of Kongo,* an artist's vision of the first encounter between Africans and their future colonizers (painted by Tshibumba Kanda Matulu, Lubumbashi, 1974); from the author's collection.

Free State contemporaries of Banza Kongo and Diogo Cão. (Stanley operated in the 1870s; Dhanis was involved in expeditions and in military campaigns between 1884 and 1893; and Bodson was killed in 1891 as a member of another expedition.)

What happened? Was the painter simply confused? Or did he, his ambition to be a modern historian notwithstanding, succumb to presumably traditional African conceptions of time according to which the remote past is presented as essentially mythical and timeless and where events are arranged not diachronically and syntagmatically as sequences, but synchronically and paradigmatically as systems consisting of significant oppositions and as equidistant from the present? Such would be an interpretation based on a structuralist analysis. Among the reservations one may have about this type of interpretation there is one that applies to the case at hand. Appeal to a timeless myth that, to evoke a structuralist idea, "thinks itself" in cultural productions dissolves contradiction, in this case between the artist's time sequence and academic chronology. I prefer to let contradiction stand, in this instance and in many others. Intended or not, because it is asserted as part of a discourse, contradiction deserves the respect we pay it when we let it disturb us. We may then seek solutions that get along without our assuming a position of higher knowledge and without explaining the problem away by logical or psychological mechanisms we could apply to our own thought only at the risk of getting caught in an infinite regress. Those who like to quote Lévi-Strauss's bon mot about anthropology being the myth of a myth have yet to tell us why that is not a myth too, and so on and so forth. As a matter of fact, to let contradiction stand because it is recognized as practical, political contradiction, and to appeal neither to universal truths nor to cultural relativity, is to me a foremost characteristic (and obligation) of a discourse on popular culture.

But I am getting ahead of the story. What Tshibumba does with chronology at this point is factually wrong. To assert this is not to exercise superior knowledge (though when two persons disagree one could, of course, be better informed than the other); it is a way of acknowledging that the painter-historian is talking about the same events and realities that academic historiography has mapped chronologically. He may, however, have different priorities and opt for different strategies, at least occasionally, in recounting what happened and when. To begin with, placing Diogo Cão and Stanley in the same time poetically challenges our received views of colonization. We tend to see fifteenth-century Portuguese discovery and subsequent rule and nineteenth-century imperialist colonization as discontinuous. or at any rate as quite different in nature. To the colonized, this distinction need not make sense; it could be more meaningful and critically more incisive to stress connections and continuity, for such an interpretation also asserts that the error in this case is not made in passing, as a matter of course. Tshibumba did not simply commit a mistake, he composed it. It is not that he got two dates wrong (in fact he does not give any dates); he made events contemporary that are separated by dates in academic chronologies. What he tries to accomplish becomes clear in his narrative that goes with the picture. There he elaborates on the inscription quoted above and adds another anachronism when he conflates yet another form of nineteenth-century colonization, that by the Arabs in the east of the country, with Portuguese discovery and Belgian occupation:

> [Banza Kongo] received Diego Cao . . . and the people who were with his party. He informed them of the name of the river. [The name] was Nzadi. Diego Cao himself called it Zaire. They did not understand each other and [when Banza Kongo said it was Nzadi] they said, yes, it is Zaire. [Diogo Cão] pronounced it Zaire. He wrote it down in his book: I discovered the river Zaire. Then [Banza Kongo] informed them about the Arabs and about those other chiefs who liked to sell their brothers. He took his time about this and began to explain to them how the Arabs conducted themselves in the interior of the Congo.

What happens here is not best understood by contrasting conceptions of time or history, generalized as cultural differences (which exist but cannot, in our case, be located here), but rather by contrasting demands of presentation. Tshibumba knew of chronology and used it in many other parts of his account. Yet he never let his inability to date an event (either exactly or at all) prevent its integration into the historical narrative. What made his account clash with academic historiography was not limited control of chronology (which is relative anyway, as I was to find out when I naively set out to establish a "correct" chronology of the history of Zaire from published sources) but the greater freedom he took—because of the greater urgency he felt—to place events where they belonged. And that kind of choice is a matter of where the narrator is placed or places himself. (Academic chronologies, again, are not in principle different. Entries always give dates and events, but what becomes an entry in a chronological list is determined by the compiler's position or chosen topic.) Certainly, in an enterprise like Tshibumba's, narration was a political act,[7] and that is one more reason to examine his ways with time pragmatically. To explore this further, let us turn now to another document of popular historiology and take a closer look at dating and placing.

Time and Timing

When I characterized historical narration as placing events where they belong, I drew on insights gained from the study of another popular historiography from Shaba, the *Vocabulary of the Town of Elisabethville* (Fabian 1990a). It was compiled a decade earlier (ca. 1965) than Tshibumba's history of Zaire (1974), is somewhat narrower in scope (concentrating on colonial history as experienced by domestic servants in the town of Elisabethville-Lubumbashi), and appeared in a different medium (it was written in a variety of Swahili adapted for literary use and mimeographed, hence destined for circulation). Apart from these and other differences, the presentations of history by the author-compiler of the *Vocabulary* and by Tshibumba (who had never seen the *Vocabulary*) agree in their broad outlines, in content and form. Taken together, the two documents convinced me that neither is idiosyncratic; they both articulate widely shared memories.

Like Tshibumba's history though less conspicuously, the *Vocabulary* reveals its ways with time when it struggles with chronology.

The matter is complex, and I can only summarize major points for this discussion (Fabian 1990a, see esp. 193–204).

Although the *Vocabulary* is a literary product that uses forms of presentation that can be realized only in writing (in a narrow sense typography, layout, and such; in a wider sense division into chapters, headings, table of contents, lists, and so on), on a scale from oral tradition to historiography it is closer to the former.

The *Vocabulary* presents sequences of events and marked periods, roughly in chronological order. Clashes and discrepancies with academic historiography are numerous. Closer examination shows that they are not random, not even occasional, such as might be expected from amateur historians. They make sense if one assumes this document is composed in a field of tension between dating a succession of events and highlighting certain events because of their significance. *Sequence* is important (a concern also expressed by the chapters' being serially numbered, 1–47), but *consequence* may take precedence in deciding where an event (or its account) should be placed in the narrative.

Collocation of events suggests that some sort of synchronic schema or paradigm was operative in organizing the overall account. Closer analysis does reveal such an architecture. Temporality in the *Vocabulary* is not conceived as a linear procession, but neither is time resorbed by mythical synchronicity. Rather, it is presented as a series of discontinuities and breaks that have their rationale in the document's conception of colonial history: accounts of colonial onslaught are followed by accounts of African resistance. An essentially political position or theme is here practically expressed in a way with time that informs the very composition of the narrative.

Another important clue to ways with time was derived from an analysis of rhetorical features in the chapter headings as well as in the text. These showed a preponderance of dialogic forms (such as question and response). And an even more intriguing trait appeared when I examined the position of chapter headings in relation to the corresponding portions of the text. Throughout the *Vocabulary* chapter headings appear to be "off" with regard to the content they announce. I described this by a musical analogy:

> At some point in a narrative or descriptive passage there occurs a break which clearly marks the introduction of a new topic. This would be the "beat." . . . Then the text is interrupted—often by multiple spacing—and the capitalized heading for the new topic follows on the off-beat . . . [I]t could be argued that there is nothing extraordinary about this. It is a convention of monographic writing to conclude one chapter with a brief outlook on, or announcement of, the next. But here the passages preceding and following the heading are in some cases almost of equal length so that the heading is placed in the middle of the topical unit it marks. (Fabian 1990a, 202–3)

There are other examples of such syncopation that cannot be discussed here. At any rate, my conclusion is that, though realized and placed typographically in a written text, these are features characteristic of oral delivery. They emphasize *timing* and performance over placement and graphic encoding. We know from thoughtful studies of "offbeat" techniques (including off-key intonation) in musical performance that they have the effect of heightening intensity and participation (see Keil 1987).

To me, all this suggests that the ways with time in popular historiography, as they appear when one concentrates on the issue of chronology, need to be understood from a perspective that transcends sterile oppositions between academic (and presumably Western) chronology and its linearity and popular (presumably African) concerns with synchronic placement. The African ways with time that are detectable in documents like these are constituted in a field of tension arising between at least three demands that authors of historical accounts must face:

dating (objectivity) placing (relevance)
timing (performance)

Presenting these three demands in a triadic relation underscores how historiology that remains committed to the performative nature of oral narration must attend to them "at the same time."

Generally, the very least this arrangement shows is that any approach to conceptions of time in other cultures is misguided if it aims only to distill cosmological ideas from whatever sources are analyzed, ideas that are then used to explain conduct (something that goes, of course, for certain theories of culture as a model or blueprint for action). Matching ideas and action (even if we assume action is mediated by institutions and social roles) simply does not catch the complexity of practices such as popular historiology.

Furthermore, there are epistemological consequences. These examples show that there is no clear dividing line between practices we designate as chronologically grounded—and often take as points of departure for comparison—and others that seem to give priority to topology, that is, to placing events in historical narratives according to culturally specific criteria of meaning or relevance. Most of all, especially in studies of time conceptions in historical consciousness that strive to be empirical, presumably objective chronologies do not anchor research to reality. Ethnography teaches us that a common ground (the practical *tertium comparationis*) can be found only in *timing*, that is, in ways with time that inform the production and performance of historical narratives.

On Performance and Representation

In the first chapter I noted an observation and a problem: it seems difficult, if not impossible, to maintain a consistent terminological distinction between popular culture and popular art. One may want to argue that culture is simply the general term, whereas art designates a subcategory. To be sure, it would sound strange if we were to call the inventors and practitioners of, say, Jamaa teaching "popular artists." Religion and art seem to be significant distinctions. No problem seems to be posed by music, theater, and painting, the other domains that have come up in these essays. But then there is the case of historiology I just discussed. Should this domain be assigned to a subcategory of, say, popular science, and should historiological modes of representation that clearly draw on poetic and rhetorical forms that are part of verbal and visual arts therefore be placed on yet a lower classificatory level as mere means of expression? And would "popular science" adequately cover (without our constantly having to point out connections with music, dance, drama, and ritual) popular practices of healing, magic, and sorcery, domains to which I paid little attention because, by circumstance rather than design, I did not focus on them as subjects of research?

There must be something about popular culture that causes us to think of it, and talk about it, as an art rather than as a science or religion of living and survival. In my own work it took me a while to realize that technical terms current in social theory—actor, role, drama—were metaphors transported from the world of theater. As far as I remember, I never gave them much thought when I was taught to use these terms as part of Parsonian "theory of action" or even when I encountered "drama" in the work of Victor Turner. Dramatist concepts were supposed to work in the analysis of social conduct precisely because they were not taken literally: actors were agents to whom values, beliefs, and motivations were imputed; roles were concepts linking individual action to social functions and institutions; drama was a notion that made it possible to conceive of social action in basically stable social systems as nevertheless dynamic. It was Turner who, complementing or further developing insights that Max Gluckman had tried to cast in seemingly contradictory terms such as "rituals of rebellion," began to break the rules of that game when he proposed that drama should be taken literally. This happened when he concluded that much of ritual action literally is performance and that therefore, epistemologically speaking, our ethnographic knowledge and our modes of representing such knowledge could profit if they too became performative. Still, I remained wary of Turner's anthropology of performance because I felt uncomfortable about what I took to be its origins, an attempt to have one's cake and eat it too: to present African societies as dynamic without giving up the idea that they were essentially repetitive, not going anywhere. Nor did I trust the wide application of Turner's ideas to all sorts of situations. I took this to be an easy escape from anthropology's obligation to a scientific discourse.

The performative nature of culture came to me as a discovery, not in a context of impressive ritual drama but as the result of a chain of events, each of them fortuitous, that led me to write *Power and Performance. Le pouvoir se mange entier,* power is eaten whole, someone had told me when I proposed to share the choice part of a meal. At the time this pronouncement needed no exegesis; only in the years that followed did I become obsessed with getting to the bottom of the matter. Was this a traditional proverb? Could I document the original version from the voluminous literature? And what exactly did it mean? My search of published collections failed to unearth an original version. At the same time, many of my urbanite friends and occasional acquaintances, some of them experts on the traditions of their ancestral cultures, unanimously expressed their conviction that *le pouvoir se mange entier* was an authentic piece of traditional wisdom. Yet not one of them was able to produce an exact counterpart in his or her native language, though not for want of trying.

I would not have been able to express this at the time, but what I had run into was a token of culture whose authenticity was affirmed, in fact experienced, every time it was pronounced, that is, performed. Yet its original version could not be produced as evidence. Finally, a group of popular actors, whom I had known for many years, responded to my question about the meaning of the phrase with the announcement that *le pouvoir se mange entier* would be the title and subject of their next show, to be discussed, rehearsed, and eventually filmed for television. It was during the first meeting-rehearsal that it dawned on me that my ethnographic search for the meaning of a presumed proverb may or may not have led me to the information I was after; it certainly prompted my respondents to articulate its meaning in performances growing from little more than affirmative or emphatic repetitions of the saying to the invention of a play around it.

I quickly drew some conclusions regarding the relative merits of "informative" versus "performative" ethnography, a distinction based on the insight that much of cultural knowledge is not available as information but needs to be enacted in performances. Today, to come back to observations I made at the beginning of this section, I realize that performance—a trait, or rather a mode, of existence of all culture—is a vital characteristic of popular culture. Though it may be literate, popular culture is not deposited in sacred or literary texts; though its artistic expressions show competence and style, there are no fixed canons, no set standards (this may go for language itself); its productions may be commodified, but there are no fixed patterns of exchange and consumption. As people lost in the dark might do, popular culture keeps talking; it needs to assure itself of its own existence by repeated performances that are unlike the routine enactments sociologists have in mind when they talk about actors and roles. Events of extraordinary intensity and quality are needed, as if to counteract the very precariousness of a form of culture that gets along without guilds of specialists, bureaucracies, or institutionalized sponsorship. Popular culture seems to exist, if not only, then predominantly, in time; places and spaces are less important to its practice than moments and events.

The conventions of ethnography, its habits of collecting information and its forms of description, make popular culture a subject difficult to study and even more so to represent. Radical departures from conventions—such as staging and performing rituals, as Victor Turner tried—are courageous. It is hard to imagine that they could adequately meet the tasks of critical interpretation and reflection that must also be part of ethnographic representation.[8] The greatest challenges remain representations that do not need to eradicate the presence of the people who have been part of producing what is being represented. Preserving and respecting presence means more than giving a voice to "informants" by citing their words and letting the reader know who they are and how they contributed to the account. Presence is about historicity, about being aware of, and addressing, among other things, historically constituted relations of power between ethnographer and interlocutors. In *Power and Performance* I tried to meet the challenges of representation as best I could by imagining and putting into practice a nonhegemonic methodology and by struggling to come up with a commensurate literary form. This, I felt, could be done only in a narrative that must not hide the narrator, since he was involved in the production of knowledge. For that reason, the account also became a narrative of self—a (partial) autobiography reporting on a slice of my life as an ethnographer.

Some of the most incisive reviewers of the book, while acknowledging, even praising, the project and its premises, felt that the narrative form, in which a self tells the story and "subsumes" an other to his purposes, in fact canceled what it was supposed to make possible: to present knowledge as a process that is actualized in events (performances) in which all participants are agents, subjects of history, rather than objects of observation.[9] Perhaps my radical intent to break with the positivist canons (of data collection, analysis, monographic presentation) raises expectations I cannot meet. More likely, I am held accountable for a dilemma that is inescapable. On the one hand, representing popular culture (specifically, not exclusively) would be misrepresenting what we know about it if we were to do it in the manner of natural history: giving tables or tableaux of presumed systems of culture—depending on whether our tastes run to the scientific or the artistic. On the other hand, trying to meet the demands of historicity by offering critical, reflexive (and therefore personal) narratives may amount to a kind of subsumption that could be taken to be even more insidious than that of objectivist, logical subsuming of data under theoretical schemes. I don't know whether anthropology will ever solve such dilemmas; in the meantime I plead for not trying to escape them by playing the old games of scientific objectivity whose apparent theoretical innocence may still hold some attraction, but only if we suppress our knowledge of practical collusion between our discipline (and others, of course) and empire in its many forms.

One thing I learned from *Power and Performance* is that being serious about popular culture, letting the labors of understanding and representation be visible, makes readers impatient. This is how one of them put it in the concluding lines of his review:

> It remains for him to "thicken" the results: to allow his own broad and deep experience in Zaire to contextualize the data. Surely we would learn more about "pouvoir" from a comparative study of pop song texts, dance steps, high fashions, wall paintings, radio ads, jokes, legends, and rumors than from this earnest (and, frankly rather tedious) compilation of texts. We need to belly up to that bar [where the idea of the play was born] and have Fabian open a Simba [beer] for us. And pass the gizzard, too. (Cosentino 1992, 117)

I'm trying. I'm trying.

4

✧ ✧ ✧

African Presence: Terrains of Contestation

African Thought and Popular Culture

> In its history, philosophy has generally been *undemocratic* (more in favor of a philosopher-king than a mass-man/woman philosopher). The African demand for an African philosophy was initially a demand to democratize, i.e. to abolish the racist-cum-social aspect of the separation between manual and intellectual labor. Is not the rejection of ethnophilosophy also a rejection of *palaver* as a genuine form of democracy-from-below? Is philosophy competent to think about democracy in Africa—if it is based on the rejection of the capacity to think of the African *people* (and not just a minority of sophisticated *catechists*)? The self-responsibilization of the African people to allow them to relate to themselves—democratization—is based on the recognition that African people think and not just on their capacity to *consume* what others have articulated.
>
> *Ernest Wamba dia Wamba*

More and more parts of Africa are receding from Western consciousness and taking their place in a vast realm of poverty, misery,

The chapter epigraph comes from a statement reproduced in the program of an international congress on Philosophy and Democracy in Intercultural Perspective, organized by the Dutch-Flemish Association for Intercultural Philosophy at Erasmus University, Rotterdam, 29–30 October 1993. Ernest Wamba dia Wamba, who was to be the keynote speaker at this meeting, was refused a visa and could not participate. Four years later he received the prestigious Prince Claus Award for Culture and Development.

and illness. They are being abandoned economically and politically because they are not interesting to this post–Cold War global economy, not even enough for exploitation and domination. Short of proposing radical changes in our industrial societies, something that is beyond hope because proposals cannot count on support even from the most enlightened, we are running out of ideas and schemes. Will Africans be able to think their way out of their present predicament? Anthropology has taught me that this is not a question of either cognitive capacities or moral fiber; as far as we can tell, both are equally distributed among human populations (so the answer would be, of course they are capable). However, politics and public opinion seem ready to set reason and morals aside for proposals advocating that the West embark, "again," on a mission to fill a void, to provide regimes of power where Africans have failed to maintain their own (Johnson 1993). The catch is in the "again." When nineteenth-century imperialists posited a void—empty geographical space and absence of civilization—it really existed as a form of their ignorance; when neoimperialists once more prepare justifications for assuming power and direct control, disguised as "humanitarian" intervention or not, they must actively ignore a vast store of knowledge that has accumulated during the past century. One would like to think that such nineteenth-century props as evolutionist racism and antislavery (meaning anti-Islam) hypocrisy could not be used again, but even that is not certain.

African studies, Africanist anthropology among them, seem to have failed if not to produce knowledge, then to establish for their knowledge the kind of presence that cannot be ignored. At the same time, creations and practices of African popular culture have achieved a global presence. African thought—if we take the term as wide enough to include artistic and religious notions and sensibilities—is alive, not only throughout Africa's Atlantic diaspora but also in the former metropolitan countries and even in some that were not involved in the colonization of Africa, at least not directly. It is not always easy to understand what that presence means and entails. I have trouble figuring out why, as was reported to me, several Japanese bands perform, in Japan, exclusively Zairian popular music in Lingala (except to guess that this must somehow be different from the well-known Japanese penchant for *Schuh-* or *Watschenplattler*, Austrian-Bavarian folk dances that are easier to demonstrate than to describe). That global neo-Pentecostalism has African or African American sources is known; that, more recently, enterprising charismatic healers and prophets from Nigeria would travel to Southeast Asia was perhaps to be expected; and that numerous communities in New York City practice vodun and pray in Yoruba seems by now altogether natural. African writers are read, and quite a few teach literature, all over the world. Ghanaian court musicians have offered regular classes in Ashanti drumming and Akan flute to American college students since the seventies. Hausa traders, their robes billowing in the breeze, sell African souvenirs (reminders of nothing more specific than the existence of Africa) on Mediterranean beaches; their colleagues spread their wares in the Paris Metro and on the sidewalks of Manhattan.

To be sure, African presence comes in vastly different forms. There is, first of all, a significant difference between a kind of presence through an astounding circulation and consumption of African images (visual as well as literary) in colonial times[1]—a form of presentation that was almost exclusively provided, certainly always framed, edited, and "acclimated" by non-Africans—and representations in which Africans have or had a decisive part. Again, the latter may range between *Présence Africaine* (the name of a journal that was prophetic at the time)[2] and *Transition,* that is, journals and groups of intellectuals that scaled the walls in which scholarly knowledge about Africa had previously been enclosed—and various African national ballets that attract large audiences in Western and Asian countries. Leading Western pop, rock, and jazz musicians have established relations with African performers that are sometimes exploitative but always creative and productive of "fusions" that are here to stay. Contemporary African sculptors and painters, including the popular painters from Zaire who figure prominently in these essays, are exhibited in galleries and museums, no longer as curiosities but as serious, challenging contributions to the art scene from Melbourne to San Francisco, from Rome to Oslo.[3] As might be expected, all this gave rise to a new critical and historical establishment, complete with specialized periodicals, regular international conferences, a vast production of books and catalogs, and academic subdisciplines.

Before I set more plates spinning than I can keep an eye on with these haphazard evocations of the global presence of African culture, I had better return to the question I started out with: Will Africans be able to think their way out of their present predicament? Although the answers are myriad—equal to African signs of life anywhere in the world—a simple yes or no is not among them. As I think about why this should be so, I realize that it is due not to an inability or refusal to predict what is going to happen (because, to cite the jargon, we are unable to control a sufficient number of variables in our calculations), but to the utter irrelevance of prediction and thinking ahead in what can never be more than an effort at thinking along with history. "Will Africans think their way out?" is a question only in its grammatical form; rhetorically it is nothing but a diffuse expression of concern, or even panic. It is, furthermore, a kind of statement that hides its true subject, which must be humanity, not only Africa. Ultimately we cannot raise the question of African survival from a spectator's point of view. Recalling an image I once used when I was asked to write a piece on the anthropology of death, we cannot entertain questions like this as if the others kept us entertained as the spectators who attended the Roman games were entertained when exotic predators tore apart their exotic victims. In our quest for knowledge and understanding, we and they are in the same arena, a view of the work of anthropology for which I have been arguing in each of the preceding chapters.

Precisely to the extent that we accept the notion of a common arena of struggle, our understanding of popular culture must aspire to a meeting of minds. To achieve this, our knowledge of what people think that thinking is and accomplishes needs to be re-represented such that it becomes present. Such presence is not established by attempts to generalize from a vast number of different expressions and practices. I doubt that we could ever portray, if such was our ambition, something like the popular African mind. But we can describe significant instances that show what Africans have in mind when, by making their contributions to popular culture, they reflect on, and talk about, thought and thinking.

Prelude: Song and Thought

A song composed and written, probably in the fifties, by Jean-Bosco Mwenda, a singer and guitar player from Shaba, begins like this:

> nikiimba
> nikiimba
> ni mawazo
> minawaza
> nakumbuka mupenzi bo

> [If I sing, If I sing, it is thought, I think, I remember (my) beloved.][4]

As I was writing this, I "thought and remembered" lines from another popular song I had commented on almost twenty years ago in the essay on African popular culture (Fabian 1978, 332):

> minaimba nawaza
> nawaza mugini
> niko naimba
> nakumbuka kwetu

✧ ✧ ✧

[I sing, I think, I think (of) the village. While I am singing I remember home.]

This song, incidentally, was the signature tune of the sketches by the Mufwankolo troupe of popular actors that were televised weekly in the mid-seventies. The program was called "Zaire ya kesho" (Zaire of tomorrow). Because of the tremendous popularity of the program, everyone in Lubumbashi, except perhaps for a few very old people and some visiting villagers, was familiar with the song. No one seemed to mind that the title of the program and the song contradicted each other. Perhaps the irony was intentional—introducing the Zaire of tomorrow with a nostalgic song from colonial times.

Be that as it may, these examples and others that could easily be found are evidence for the wide acceptance of *kuwaza,* to think, and *kukumbuka,* to remember, as elements of popular thought. That in this case they occur in sentimental and nostalgic song-poems in no way undermines what I shall assert presently about the weight that is given to "thought" in a discourse that "remembers" as a form of contestation. The love songs of the late forties and the fifties (that is, the earliest documented on recordings) often were laments, addressed by thwarted or abandoned male lovers or husbands to women bearing French names (Stephanie and Chérie Veronique in my examples). That they were veiled complaints about colonial relations was obvious to all but the colonizers. As in popular historiology, in popular song thinking and remembering were a way of recalling pain, humiliation, and separation, on the personal as well as the political level. Little has changed in postcolonial times. Today, songs about male-female relations still seem to be the safest, yet most effective, way of thinking aloud about relations and abuses of power without getting caught (at least most of the time).[5]

Humanism: Jamaa and the Recuperation of Dignity

Against this background evoked by popular song, I now want to examine several contexts in which thought—as a concept whose meaning must be sought in a field of tension between reasoning and remembering—became a focus of inquiry in my own research.

When I first encountered the Jamaa (in 1966–67), people were still close to the traumatic events of Congolese independence (in 1960) and the upheavals that followed. I was too caught up in theories of acculturation, modernization, and social change to realize just how much the Jamaa, like other movements of its kind, was about overcoming the traumas of colonization. Though I accepted "movement" as a categorization (and thereby the connotation of the term as something ephemeral and transitional), I assumed that these experiences could and should studied because they represented intellectual and emotional efforts that needed to be understood in and on their own terms. I still think the best studies of African religious movements have been those that did not make their object into an epiphenomenon, a function derivative of economic or political necessities.[6]

At a time when social scientists, while deploring the speed and violence of change, reluctantly acknowledged "independency" as a motive behind African religious enthusiasm, movements in Zaire responded to the necessity of coming to grips with the demise of a paternalist regime and with new forms of political relations and power that existed in popular consciousness as "independence." Since the fifties, some observers had argued that African religious movements were incipient political movements, or political movements in disguise (depending on whether they were viewed in an evolutionary or a revolutionary perspective).[7] Neither interpretation would have fit the Jamaa of the fifties and sixties. Still, based on what we know today about symbolic power under Belgian colonial rule and about the uncomfortable position the movement's founder, Placide Tempels, occupied in the colonial regime, the

Jamaa appears to have been a timely form of confrontation with the Catholic mission church, the institution in which most of the colony's instruments and resources of symbolic power were concentrated at the time.

Less obvious, at least to me, was that this movement also made a gesture of distancing itself from the sociopolitical context of the African working class in Katanga. Since the turn of the century, when colonization effectively got under way in this region, a rather peculiar situation had developed. An all-powerful mining company (Union Minière du Haut Katanga), sustained by an equally powerful land- and concessions-holding institution (Comité Spécial du Katanga, CSK), had established a "state within a state." The very premise of that arrangement—private commercial interests pursued in the guise of government—made the integration of Katanga into the Belgian colonial state precarious. Tensions and contradictions intensified after independence when, termination of the CSK and nationalization of the mining industry notwithstanding, the old opposition between central colonial administration and local industry and commerce turned into a struggle between national and foreign interests. Such a situation is not unique, and that may make the Jamaa movement all the more interesting as evidence for popular political thought.

As directed against the mission church, the "gesture of distancing" entailed this: The Jamaa was at first hailed by the progressive clergy as a lay movement giving proof of the maturity of African Christians. When it turned out that this "commendable initiative" was indeed an organization in which members of the church hierarchy had no position of privilege or power, and when attempts to assert clerical control were resisted, it did not take long before there were clashes with the clergy (foreign as well as African). Since the late sixties, the mission church has tried to regain control of a movement that at one time seemed to attract a majority of its active believers. By now the struggle has been going on for more than thirty years. As we saw in chapter 2, it has not been resolved in any one consistent way. Parts of the Jamaa have formally separated from the Catholic Church (although they adopted the legal status of an independent church under protest). Others formally accepted control by the church hierarchy in rituals of abjuration and submission. Yet other groups chose to do neither and to continue as before, ignoring excommunication and other sanctions.

What is the evidence that contestatory thought caused the Jamaa to seek confrontation with one of the most powerful colonial institutions? From the point of view of the mission, this movement's move toward confrontation was no move at all, but a case of error, heresy, ill-conceived syncretism, and adopting dubious moral (sexual) practices. Measures of control were taken, including mass excommunication, yet the Jamaa refused to separate from the church. I argued long ago that this peculiar form of "unseparated separatism" was made possible by a doctrine that can best be characterized as a radical humanism. Jamaa teachings go back to Placide Tempels's *Bantu Philosophy,* an ideological manifesto that seems to have lost none of its original attractiveness.[8] As developed in the *mafundisho* of the Jamaa, the instructions leading up to initiation, Tempels offered an edifice of ideas and ways of reasoning that were radical—especially in their radical affirmation of equality among sexes, races, and social classes—without being explicitly political. Jamaa ideas were enacted by initiation and other activities within the movement, not by any outside agitation for, say, equal rights.

Above all, Jamaa thought was metaphysical, concerned with the deepest foundations of doctrine. Its central tenets made it possible to value traditional beliefs (for instance, regarding health and fecundity) and to embrace Catholic teaching on a level that identified deep commonalities. In this way the Jamaa avoided, by and large, outright confrontation between traditional beliefs and Christian doctrine. Thus, although the movement offered a picture of Christians' having abandoned pagan beliefs and practices and having firmly accepted the teachings of Catholic theology, it was in reality an ingenious form of intellectual and moral survival amid the pressures of reified tradition and institutionalized religion. An all-pervasive preoccupation with *bumuntu*—what it really means, and takes, to be a human being—had made secondary, if not irrelevant, the problem of neatly sorting out pagan and Christian religious beliefs and practices. Recuperation of human dignity (rather than salvation) had become the focus of doctrine and ritual.

This concern with dignity also inspired the gesture of distancing that the Jamaa made against its immediate social and political environment. Almost from the beginning, observers noticed the movement's lack of interest in social issues and its disdain for political action. Hardly a trace of class solidarity, let alone militancy, could be detected in this organization that originated and spread almost exclusively among workers. Yet in some of its central teachings, the Jamaa did in fact contest and counteract social policies that had been vital to industrial operations in Katanga-Shaba.[9] Among them was, first, the hierarchical distribution of gender roles among male wage earners and female reproducers of the labor force. The Jamaa not only affirmed absolute (but complementary) equality of the sexes in its doctrine, it also promoted sharing of resources, responsibilities, and leisure activities in daily practice. As a rule, only married couples could become members of the movement. Second, labor recruitment and labor management (including policies guiding settlement and mobility) had always promoted (exploited, manipulated) ethnic distinctions and divisions. In Jamaa teaching, *bumuntu* had two lethal enemies: *bupeke,* pursuit of selfish interests by an individual alone, and *bukabila,* tribalism and racism. It now begins to dawn on me that the movement's insistence on redefining "human being" as essentially a twosome (Fabian 1979d) may have been not so much an attempt to utilize presumptive Bantu thought to shore up Christian marriage as a conceptual device designed to preempt class and ethnic (but also church or denominational) identification, which presupposes individuals as members or carriers of attributes. Even though it may never have had much of a chance against the combined forces of Christian salvation and capitalist exploitation, Tempels's Bantu philosophy, as transformed into Jamaa *mawazo,* thought, was correctly perceived as a threat by the colonial and postcolonial powers. Mobutu Sese Seko, it was reported, thought highly of Tempels as someone who anticipated his doctrine of *authenticité.* Nevertheless, under his regime clergy, mining company, and army cooperated nicely during the virulent phase of "solving the problem of the Jamaa" in the mid-seventies.

Prayer and Ecstasy: Charismatics and the Spirit of Despair

From all we know, the Jamaa has become a minor player on the current religious and political stage. The political significance of the popular philosophy that this seemingly apolitical movement developed as its intellectual, perhaps intellectualist, response to the challenge of decolonization is perhaps best appreciated when contrasted with ideas guiding the Charismatic Renewal that emerged in the seventies and has come to play a major role in the agony of Zaire. In terms the two movements themselves use to define what they are about, the Jamaa *thinks,* charismatics *pray*. Jamaa gnosis (a possible translation of *mawazo),* however hermetic and introverted, has been conceived as a philosophical vision with a humanist perspective. Jamaa often defined itself, collectively, as searching for a way (*kutafuta njia).* Charismatics do not search for the Holy Spirit; they wait and pray to be "filled" by its power. Prayer (*sala*), as it is promoted by the charismatics, appears to lack reflection as well as projection of a goal. Charismatic prayer is not really begging for something (*kuomba*); it is praise (*sifa*), ideally expressed in a bodily state of rapture (in voice, posture, movement, often leading to a kind of trance that resembles an epileptic seizure). The same abandonment of conscious intent and purpose seems to happen in charismatic glossolalia when speech loses referential and discursive functions and becomes proof of the presence of the Spirit. There is something desperate in charismatic enthusiasm. The conclusion I came to after a brief but intensive period of research among

Lubumbashi prayer groups can be put, somewhat flippantly, as follows: Charismatics engage in the kind of prayer you take to when you haven't got a prayer.

One could argue that emphasis on the body is not what distinguishes charismatics from the Jamaa. In the latter, ritualized demonstrations of sexual love as tokens of spiritual life and fecundity certainly played an important role. But the fixation on the body among the charismatics—witness, for instance, the all-pervasive concern with health and healing—manifests itself in something that was consciously rejected and controlled in the Jamaa: the central importance accorded in charismatic practice to various forms of possession, either as demonstrations of the Spirit or as evidence for the presence of evil spirits and forces. Discernment of spirits and exorcism are practiced in prayer groups as a matter of routine, and both practices go together with an ardent rejection of magic and sorcery that, as many observers have noted, implies recognizing their existence and real force. Charismatics in Zaire address their practices to forms of power and to powers that be that are different from the ones the Jamaa faced during late colonial and early postcolonial times. They respond to, participate in, a political culture that has been characterized as governed by the "politics of the belly" (Bayart 1993, originally 1989). We must get used to the thought that magic and sorcery can be central in a thoroughly modern society.

The Charismatic Renewal has had amazing success in Zaire, as well as elsewhere in Africa and the world.[10] It should be clear by now that I take a dim view of its critical, emancipatory potential. But I certainly would not want to close the book on questions regarding relations between Shaba prayer groups and the international charismatic movement, between the local and the global and the relation of both to popular culture. I would like to know more about the women who have led popular opposition to Mobutu's regime in Kinshasa, and even engaged in open clashes with it. Many of them, I was told, were leaders of prayer groups. It is also likely that links and connections established through the Charismatic

Renewal (especially in its more sedate, internationally oriented, middle-class circles) may have helped to establish networks of political opposition.[11] Still, in the current situation of Zaire, charismatic prayer seems to "work" by turning despair into ecstasy. For great numbers of Zairians, such prayer has become a way to cope. But is religious ecstasy any more likely to open new spaces for freedom and rational discourse than the "dance on the volcano" that large parts of the bourgeois elite have been performing?

In the absence of recent information about developments among prayer groups, it is impossible to offer more than guesses, based on what I saw (and others reported) in the eighties. There was evidence that several of the leaders and probably many members of prayer groups were recruited from the Jamaa. Even a cursory examination of the recordings of prayer meetings I made in the mid-eighties shows that these recruits brought along their rhetorical habits (including more than just fragments of Jamaa doctrinal language). There are, in other words, connections to the Jamaa (and presumably to other movements, such as the Legio Mariae, that also lost members to the prayer groups), and if my view of the origins and context of the Jamaa is correct, to local popular culture. It was also obvious to me that the efforts of the mission church to co-opt the global charismatic movement (in the form of a hierarchically organized national Renouveau headed by Jesuit priests) did little to change the collision course most local charismatic leaders had embarked on. Several (former) Zairian priests who had defied their bishops' orders to desist from charismatic practices became folk heroes, symbols of popular resistance. With their emphasis on spirit healing and exorcism of evil forces, prayer groups (even though they varied considerably with respect to explicitness in these matters) had become major agencies of protection against sorcery. In fact there were more than just intimations[12] in the reports I had that for many members of the upper class and the political establishment prayer groups were *the* major alternative to the complicated, risky, and expensive measures of magic protection that everyone,

Mobutu more than others, felt it necessary to take. This would mean that prayer groups became conduits for these persons to rejoin and stay in touch with strategies of survival chosen by the people. All this adds up to a picture that confirms what I said earlier about the dialectical relation between local and global. They are connected to global Catholic neo-Pentecostalism; as a form of local survival, Zairian prayer groups should be counted among the inventions and expressions of popular culture.

Realism: Popular Memory and Historiology

When I noted contrasts between religious responses to late colonial and postcolonial situations (thought, in the case of the Jamaa) and to a kind of terminally postcolonial situation (prayer, in the case of the charismatics), I did not hide my sympathies for thought. Nor do I deny that this implies taking a political position. The never-ending descent of countries like Zaire into poverty and violence makes it difficult to maintain a detached, purely scientific sense of purpose in our attempts to produce knowledge about them. What keeps me going is the conviction—adding another twist to the question asked at the beginning of this chapter—that the only hope a people has is to think itself out of its present plight. By this I do not mean that something like African philosophy will accomplish the task; it takes intellectual and artistic innovations that can become shared practices of coping, roughly what my francophone colleagues would call *savoir populaire.*[13] Some of these creations and practices, notably popular music and to a lesser extent theater (especially when broadcast on television), have reached practically everyone in the towns and villages of Zaire; others may as yet be only emerging or may be inconspicuous to the outsider, especially when they are not expressed in a single medium.

Among the inconspicuous forms of *savoir populaire* is popular historiology,[14] told, written, painted, and (en)acted. Historio*graphy* is too narrow a designation of popular concern with history. It does justice neither to its metahistorical (theoretical as well as poetic) dimensions nor to the multitude of media in which it is expressed (writing, oral narrative, dramatic and musical performance, and painting). Like others who have seriously studied the documents produced by this form of popular thought,[15] I consider the making of histories the political cutting edge of popular culture, a "terrain of contestation" if there ever was one. As it turns out, *kuwaza* and *mawazo,* the *thinking of,* and *thoughts about,* history are key concepts in the two remarkable documents that I introduced in the preceding chapter: the *Vocabulary of the Town of Elisabethville* (Fabian 1990b) and Tshibumba's history of Zaire (Fabian 1996). The mimeographed text of the *Vocabulary* was dated September 1965, a few months before I began research on the Jamaa (and before Mobutu established his regime through a military coup), Tshibumba's history was produced and recorded in the final few months of my last extensive stay in Shaba (1974).

The *Vocabulary,* recall, is a history of colonization written by the colonized for the colonized. I titled my interpretive essay on this document "Thoughts against Suffering" because this seemed to summarize what the text had to say about the nature of historical experience and the rationale for producing this account. Though not employed frequently, *kuwaza,* the verb, and especially *mawazo,* the noun, were found to have a key function in this document. Here is how I stated one of my conclusions: "*Mawazo* is here employed to designate the genre of our text: in its entirety, although it contains elements of many other genres, the *Vocabulary* is thus designated as *reflection,* as 'philosophical,' that is, reasoned rather than 'mere' history, somewhat in the sense in which this term was used by the Enlightenment since Voltaire" (Fabian 1990a, 183). Another insight that has had our attention (earlier in this chapter and in chapter 2) and will be taken up again later is the close association of *kuwaza-mawazo* with *kukumbuka* and its derivations. *Ukumbusho,* that which makes (one) remember, was the collective-abstract term designating the purpose and nature of Shaba genre painting. Looking at its meaning in the *Vocabulary,* I found that the various occurrences were not so much referring to memories (as recorded in the text) as voicing "active appeals, calling on the readers to remember. The *Vocabulary* is not a memory but a reminder" (ibid., 188). I cited a passage that occurs toward the end of the document where the author(s) exhort the readers: "We cannot show all this in a few words. Everyone knows about it, it is *kukumbusha tu akili yetu,* just to remind us so that we think of it [literally, to make our mind or intelligence recall (it)]" (ibid.).

Kuwaza and *mawazo* were equally central, but more explicitly discussed, in recorded conversations I had with the author of the second document, or set of documents, dating from the mid-seventies. This is the history of Zaire as painted and told by the Shaba popular painter Tshibumba Kanda Matulu. André Yav, the author-compiler of the *Vocabulary,* stays in the background as a writer and remains de facto anonymous. So far we know almost nothing about him except his name and the fact that his ethnic origin and political orientation were Lunda. Tshibumba foregrounded his authorship by signatures and inscriptions on the pictures, as well as by statements in his narrative and reflections. He defined himself as an artist-historian and declared *mawazo* and *kuwaza,* thought and thinking, to be the essence of both his painting and his historiology. This is amply documented and commented on in the ethnographic work on his history of Zaire.[16] Here I quote a passage from our conversations that preceded the actual narrative. It contains statements that at first seem to contradict what I have said about thought and critical contestation. In an attempt to get Tshibumba to name his own criteria and standards, I had shown him a painting by Ilunga Beya, a less accomplished genre painter (fig. 3). He had reservations, and when we discussed Ilunga's use of colors, Tshibumba made a surprising statement:

Fabian. But what about the colors?
Tshibumba. The colors, you say? Yes, he mixes, but [with a

3. *The Bush,* a genre of popular painting that serves as a reminder of the past (painted by Ilunga Beya, Lubumbashi, 1973); from the author's collection.

chuckle] he is just learning. But we don't reject this because among artists, in art, there is no critique.

F. There is no critique in art?

T. In art, you don't criticize your fellow artist.

F. This is not allowed?

T. No. Just look, the ideas he realizes, they are good. But the people who look at it may offer critique, yes, or those who are knowledgeable, a professor like you, [or] someone who was trained at an academy.

F. Mm.

T. But we—there are some I meet whose work I consider good.

F. Mm. But, within the group of artists you cannot criticize?

T. No, I cannot criticize a thing made by [another] person because it is thought that is at work and he struggles for progress

in this thought. What I can do is to help him with this thought, if it is there.
F. So this is how it is: All of you, each artist just works by himself?
T. We artists work by ourselves, through our thoughts.
F. I see.
T. What counts is that I come up with a good result.
F. So you cannot improve another person?
T. Ah, no, I can improve someone else.
F. You can?
T. I said I can improve someone else.
F. But without criticizing?
T. That's it, no critique. He can be counseled if you have advice.

Tshibumba affirmed the fundamental premise of his work: Thought is the source of artistic creation in general, and of this particular project of a history of his country. On many occasions he insisted that his intent was to critically confront other, official versions of the history of Zaire. When he recognized critique as a privilege of specialized practitioners ("professors"), this was a nod to something that high culture does not seem able to do without. Within his own practice he admitted no supposedly objective canon of rules or standards, other than the wisdom and counsel the experienced give to neophytes. But that does not mean he thought of that practice as free of conflict and strife. When I asked him, at another moment in our conversation, whether the painters of Shaba ever thought of getting organized, Tshibumba told me that no such association existed:

F. Why is that?
T. It's because there is no mutual understanding among us, as I told you before.
F. But what is the reason?
T. It is because we do not communicate, we don't even agree that we should set up an association.

F. So there is no mutual understanding?

T. There is some to the point where you can go to a fellow artist and talk with him.

F. Yes.

T. But then you go home.

F. Fine, but . . .

T. But there is no agreement on rules.

F. Mm.

T. To say, look, this is the work we do, let's work together in one house which then could turn into a gallery and that is how we will make progress and become big—this sort of thing does not exist.

F. And why is that?

T. I think it is greed for money. I don't know. Let's say, if we were to put our money together, there would always be one who has the power, and he will take it all.

What remained implicit about critique among painters in the first fragment quoted is here spelled out: to be critical, a painter must assume, share, and contest "power within," a notion I introduced and discussed in chapter 2. Even under the conditions that gave rise to genre painting as a domain of popular culture (among which "money"—greed for and chronic lack of—may be the most pervasive), it is thought that creates and thought that contests; Tshibumba leaves no doubt about that. It would be wrong to have the expectation that tempts many of us who have read Jürgen Habermas—that communicative practices that resist and contest power ill gained should be themselves power free. In Tshibumba's experience, popular painters communicate rarely and never like to share power. As a painter, historian, and thinker, he is a realist.

Thought and the Creation of Terrains of Contestation

I will return to the issue of power, but first let us look at what we have gained so far from approaching popular culture as thought.

Thought and thinking are common and central themes. A striking convergence can be observed between Jamaa teaching, poetry in popular music, the recording of colonial memories in the *Vocabulary*, and their translation into painted images and narrative in the history of Zaire. The documents that support this view were produced in the same area, by people, and for audiences, belonging to the same population and social class. Convergence therefore is not an accident. It is, I believe, proof of an established common practice of creating an intellectual, discursive space in which critical consciousness can be stated, communicated, and debated, which is what I had in mind when I spoke of terrains of contestation in the title of this chapter.[17]

Anticipating the objection that this puts an intellectualist, hence practically and politically doubtful or irrelevant, interpretation on popular thought, I shall offer some observations. Even though my evidence covers a relatively short period—three decades if we count from the formulation of Jamaa doctrine, preceded by *Bantu Philosophy* in the mid-forties, to Tshibumba's historiology in the mid-seventies—it is clear that popular concern with *mawazo* has been not a uniform ideological reflex but a process of conception and elaboration that produced strikingly different results. The followers of the Jamaa—who, incidentally, would sometimes call themselves "guardians of *mawazo*"—opted for a closed and ritualized doctrine, a *gnosis*.[18] Perhaps closure was inevitable, given the specific religious situation in which they constituted their terrain of contestation. In the long run, it nevertheless limited and all but neutralized the broader political impact this particular practice of *mawazo* might have had. In the popular historiologies, emphasis on thought and thinking promoted a strikingly open, realistic, nonideological concern with history as a means of coming to grips with the present.

Perhaps there remain doubts regarding the practical impact of *mawazo*. Even if my interpretation of the concept's discursive, critical importance is correct, one may ask just how representative these documents are of popular thought about thought and thinking. Three principal reasons make me assert that they are representative. First, even though Jamaa teachings about *mawazo* are part of a hermetic doctrine, whereas Tshibumba's reflections are those of a creative intellectual (with the *Vocabulary* occupying some point between those two extremes), in all three instances thought and thinking are directed to issues and experiences that are shared by the population of, at least, urban-industrial Shaba. Second, to a large extent such sharing of experience, as well as a conceptual approach to experience, is made possible by the semantics of *mawazo* and *kuwaza* (and that of related terms such as *kujua,* to know, *kukumbuka,* to think of, to remember) in a common linguistic medium, Shaba Swahili. Third, in the contexts and documents we are considering here, the semantics of *mawazo* and *kuwaza* includes connotations wider than the simple gloss "to think" suggests. *Kuwaza* can signify dreaming and imagining (the usual terms are *kulota,* to dream, and *ndoto,* dream). This is most literally so in Jamaa teaching, where *mawazo* also refers to the dreams that are required to ascertain that candidates are ready to be initiated. At one crucial point in his history, Tshibumba also identified a dream as *mawazo* and as the source of one of his most powerful, visionary paintings of the future of his country (fig. 4). *Mawazo* can be embodied thought—a story, a historical narrative, but also a picture. Jamaa discourse and popular historiology make use of widely shared cultural resources, such as traditional animal stories, popular legends, songs, and anecdotes. Even Tshibumba's pictorial work, though in many respects unique, is firmly grounded in Shaba genre painting and shares its declared purpose—*kukumbusha,* to make people remember.

There is, of course, an important difference between Jamaa *mawazo* and the thoughts expressed in popular historiology. Although the Jamaa made gestures of distancing that were realistic in that they addressed an actual situation, it opted for a closed doctrine that tended to be philosophically abstract and contained a strong mythical orientation (for instance, in a dualist distinction between a visible and an invisible world). Neither ideological closure nor mythification characterizes popular historiology. From years of pon-

4. *Mysterious Dream of the Artist,* a popular artist's prophetic vision of the end of the Mobutu era (painted by Tshibumba Kanda Matulu, Lubumbashi, 1974); from the author's collection.

dering documents such as the *Vocabulary,* the various genres that made up Shaba popular painting, and especially Tshibumba's pictures of the history of Zaire, I take away the impression of a thoroughly realistic attitude toward history and the present. This is not limited to a preponderance of, say, narrative prose, telling "how things happened," or of realistic representation in the paintings. Above all, it is expressive of an epistemological realism. The authors of these historiologies, individually or collectively, place themselves in concrete space and time—their present predicament in Zaire—and claim authority as witnesses or compilers of testimony. They do not write or paint as (im)passive chroniclers; they are "thinkers" who realize that history is made, not found. They make bold statements, yet they also experience uncertainty and admit the possibility of error (see my observations on chronology in the preceding chapter), which they may express in their narratives and reflections. Doubts and disclaimers were not part of Jamaa teaching and certainly not of the doctrinal system. If at all, they surfaced in exceptional, liminal situations. When they make use of official historiography, popular historians do so critically. Often, received accounts and interpretations of historical events are cited only to be contested. Even when they incorporate sources that have the generic traits of legends, of allegoric or fantastic stories, they do this in a manner of collage that in no way diminishes the overall realistic effect. In a society in which dreams and practices we would classify as magic are part of daily life, it would be unrealistic to filter them out from accounts of shared experiences and memories. But perhaps the most striking indicator of realism is the conscious and explicit way the authors address relations of political power; not only those that make the stuff of history, but also those that determine and constrain historiology. Irony, parody, allusion, and ellipsis are often resorted to. The very operation of these figures and rhetorical strategies attests to a political intent to criticize and contest.

Anarchy and Democratization?

So far I have tried to sketch varying contexts in which conscious reflection on, and explicit talk about, thought and thinking creates terrains of contestation. Now I shall take this discussion back to questions that were the starting point of this chapter: What do we know about thought, about power on the local level, as it is understood "from the bottom up," and how can such knowledge help us gauge the capacity of popular thought to overcome the present situation? What, to address one of the issues that has figured prominently in recent debates, are the prospects for democratization in Africa?[19]

During periods of varying length that followed the granting of independence—all of them brief on the time scale that measures, for instance, African popular culture—African nation-states were constituted as republics with democratic institutions. Almost all of them came to be ruled by military dictators and the often changing power elites these leaders were able to co-opt. As these regimes begin to crumble, after having robbed their countries blind and exhausted their international political capital, it seems logical not only that power should "revert to the people," but that this should happen through constitutions and institutions that are democratic as defined by Euramerican legal and political thought. Remember also that this sort of foregone conclusion has in the past been powerfully supported by an evolutionary perspective according to which democracy represents the inevitable outcome of a process of rationalization, provided that a society or nation has reached a corresponding level of socioeconomic development. This view often went together with psychological evaluations that in the past, but again in recent days, invoked concepts such as maturity and the will to seek self-government. The terms are familiar from a phase in discussions of the "colonial question" when political independence for Africans could be discussed academically—that is, when one could talk and write about Africans' being primitive and childlike without having to call them that to their face, simply because one never came into situations where one had to face Africans on an equal footing. As far as I can recall, in the "new nations" debates of thirty years ago, evolutionary and psychological notions, if entertained at all, were kept in the background. Voluntarist attitudes were assumed, whereby political maturity became a matter of modernizing and changing within cultural frames that, though also changing, were seen as cultural traditions providing direction and relative stability. If, as I sense it, evolutionary laws and (individual) psychology seem to appeal once again to many who talk about democratization today, this is a return to colonial discourse without the excuses its original version may have had. Today there is nothing we can conceivably pronounce about Africans that is not also said to their faces.

Against these assumptions and expectations, it becomes extremely difficult first to recognize and then to represent popular thought that contests, or perhaps simply ignores, ready-made models of democracy. However, unless what motivates this discussion is nothing but proselytizing for our forms of government, we must consider that democratization, understood as political thought and action emanating from the people, cannot be equated with the introduction of democratic institutions and forms of government. For one thing, it should be obvious by now that political development in Africa may not be linear-evolutionary but may run in cycles in which autocratic and democratic phases alternate.

Having named what I believe to be obstacles to appreciating popular political thought, let me now turn again to some reflections on what I counted as a substantial finding in my studies both of the more recent fate of the Jamaa movement (Fabian 1994) and of thought about power in popular wisdom as it is expressed in proverbs and popular theater (Fabian 1990b). I shall now put up for discussion a thesis derived from two observations. One was the dispersal, in fact dissipation, of charismatic authority (taking "charismatic" in its sociological, Weberian meaning) in the Jamaa. By the mid-eighties, the name referred to at least four types of Jamaa, a "diversification" that itself occurred against the background of an astounding proliferation of movements, cults, and churches. The other observation resulted from an analysis of the practical consequences of conceptualizations of power I had found expressed in the key axiom that got me started on my project: *le pouvoir se mange entier,* power is eaten whole. Both observations led me to assert the following hypothesis:

> What looks to us at first like dissipation of power in the stronger, or diversification in the weaker meaning, may not be indicative of forced adaptation to external circumstances of post-colonial political economy, much less of internal disintegration and decline. It may be the very form in which a particular cultural notion of power realizes itself. What looks

> paradoxical or simply confusing from the outside—the ardent pursuit of power in its entirety and the proliferation of its embodiments—may express a cultural preference for a state of anarchy, be it in religion, economics, or politics. (Fabian 1994, 271–72)[20]

The core of *Power and Performance* was a theatrical play conceived to elaborate the meaning of *le pouvoir se mange entier.* It was developed around a deceptively simple plot, set in an imaginary village. A chief proclaims rules of proper conduct and issues orders for communal work. The villagers, corrupted by venal elders, refuse to obey. They commit individual offenses and eventually defy the chief in a communal orgy of drinking and dancing in the fields outside the village. There is chaos. The chief sends out his elders to restore order, to no avail. In the end he himself confronts the villagers, deposes the notables, and takes all the power into his own hands. However, and here I must refer to the book for the detail of the argument, one would misunderstand what happened in this performance (of which preparatory discussions, rehearsals, and later comments were an integral part) if one were to take it as a simple morality play asserting the necessity of order and control. If anything it was an enactment of an essentially anarchic conception of power (see Fabian 1990b, 258–61).

Combining insights gleaned from *Power and Performance* with what I learned from the study of charismatic authority and popular historiology, I come to a conclusion that will probably be perceived as scandalous: *Political anarchy must be seriously considered as a realistic option for, and outcome of, "democratization,"* if the term is to mean political thought and action from the bottom up rather than just the importing or imposing of institutions whose history, after all, has been inseparable from capitalist and imperialist expansion.[21] Therefore it is not unrealistic, or a mere escape into nostalgia, when Africans express regrets about independence and blame it for their present predicament. I call anarchy a realistic option because it is supported by deep-seated cultural conceptualizations of the nature of political power and by sustained, rational efforts to understand present difficulties as the outcome of a shared history.

Anarchy as a rational option is emphatically not to be confused with pseudorealistic analyses of a factual breakdown and descent into Hobbesian chaos demanding brutal outside response in the form of outright intervention and ultimately political recolonization. Nor could anarchy be a rational option if it were conceived in mere negative terms—as the absence of effective government. It should be thought of as a discursive terrain of contestation, and it will be up to Africans—the people as well as those certified intellectuals who think from and for the people—to invent or reinvent models and institutions of political life that make possible survival with dignity. Outsiders, no matter how perceptive and well informed, often take shortcuts. To cite but one example, Michael Schatzberg's proposal to consider "father and family" as truly indigenous models of political relations (1993) is a far cry from the kind of institution mongering that we often get from political science. The problem I nevertheless have with this and similar arguments is that metaphors—expressed, for instance, when African leaders claim fatherhood of their nation or some sort of traditional chiefhood—are not reversible; they do not support the conclusion that Africans yearn for a father or a chief as political leader. More important, the search for traditional models that may serve as future alternatives tends to ignore the resources Africans have in popular culture. In the documents of popular thought I have discussed here, discourse about power may center on metaphors (such as the connection between power and eating), but its overall intent tends to be realistic. Metaphors, after all, can be a realistic means of stating actual relations under conditions of political repression.

Finally, it should be obvious that I am not assigning anarchic democratization to Africans. Ernest Wamba dia Wamba—who has for many years been working on the palaver, communal litigation, as a viable form of dealing with power—points out, in the same statement with which I prefaced this chapter, that "democracy must be conceptualized at the level of the whole planet Earth." If anarchy is a realistic option of democratization, it may have to be considered globally. I think that, in a time where once comfortable compartmentalizations and distinctions between democratic and nondemocratic societies are getting blurred, few need to be convinced that this is so. Therefore serious thought about Africa, and study of democratization there, is anything but a matter of bringing ready solutions to that continent. Democratization as a solution is the problem.

5

✧ ✧ ✧

Conclusion

First a reminder of a remote but commanding reason that made me embark on these reflections. As an anthropologist, I face a specific form of what is probably a general quandary. Let me call it the paradox of enslaving liberation. As I understand the history of my discipline, there can be no doubt that the idea of culture started out as a conceptualization of freedom: freedom from ignorance, from greed and need, from habit and custom, indeed from nature. Even when, during the Enlightenment, theories of culture emerged that stressed determination by natural law, such determinism (as we must also grant to many evolutionists and latter-day cultural materialists) was pronounced proof of scientific freedom's overcoming superstition. But freedom as an idea does not equal freedom as praxis, and the actual history of culture theory in anthropology has been anything but a history of liberation. On the whole we must realize, with the benefit of hindsight (if benefit is the right term, since the idea is depressing), that anthropological theorizing, though it has perhaps not always supported Western colonial and imperial expansion, has often colluded with it.

Thinking about popular culture in Africa has caused me again and again to point out the shortcomings of "received culture theory." I used this phrase to refer to the anthropological theory of culture as it informed the paradigm that reigned during its modern phase, structuralism-functionalism. The formulations Clifford Geertz gave to it in his several essays on religion, ideology, commonsense, or art "as a cultural system" (1973, chaps. 4 and 8; 1983, chaps. 4 and 5) have been obligatory references in anthropological writing ever since. Lest what is given here as an example of received culture theory be misunderstood as a dismissal of his work, however, let me point out that Geertz, more consciously and successfully than others, deployed his culture concept for much the same reasons that make me talk about popular culture: it allowed him to understand, indeed perceive, matters concerning religion and such that other disciplines, or other approaches in anthropology, ignored. Also, he was never afraid to deal with the messy aspects of contemporary culture in the societies he studied.

Nonetheless, from the perspective of these essays, the discourse on popular culture was conceived to contest what I have called culture *tout court* because—much like what it describes—it is seen to contest high culture. It is easy to qualify, perhaps dismiss, such critique of culture as populist, that is, as motivated by political, even demagogic interests. But an apolitical position is—objectively, if not subjectively—not attainable as long as the sciences we pursue are human practices. Siding with the people, devoting time, energy, and a large part of one's life to understanding what is being created "in low places," should not be something an anthropologist needs to feel defensive about. Political, partisan commitment, however, is not what ultimately gives strength to arguments based on the study of popular culture. Such arguments, if they are to be arguments rather than gratuitous counterstatements, must share a common ground with the positions they criticize. Common ground, in this case, means basic ideas and terms that are accepted within the discipline of anthropology. Who would want to raise his or her voice for a topic such as popular culture, who would want to listen to what is said about it, if to belong to a discipline did not also mean to be assured of an audience and to be recognized as a speaker? Common ground, of course, can also exist between disciplines and, a more urgent matter of concern, between anthropology and those we study.

On the subject of common ground, advocating a concept of popular culture in opposition to that of high culture is often misunderstood as putting a choice before us. Either deny unity, purity, stability, authority, and refinement as describing high culture and be able to perceive and appreciate plural, mixed, unstable, contestatory, slipshod popular culture, or make popular culture the standard-ideal type and denounce the rarefied nature of high culture. This is a misleading presentation of the question. Unity, purity, and so on cannot be denied where they are real; they must be rejected where they become criteria defining what counts as real. That is why the *opposition* between high culture and popular culture does not derive from the nature of whatever things we have in mind when we *distinguish* the two: Why should a concerto grosso be oppressive to a rock musician? Why a Rembrandt to Tshibumba? Either becomes oppressive only when it is wielded as a weapon by powers that must oppress in order to stay in power.

Although it is important to remember all this, I still needed to pinpoint the crucial issue, the source of dissatisfaction that made me embark on these reflections. By retracing in these essays the steps that led me from the study of a religious movement to inquiries into popular language, theater, painting, and to a lesser extent other expressions such as music and material culture, I have tried to show that a concept of popular culture was necessary to make visible, to constitute as objects of research, vast portions of contemporary African life that received culture theory *and* established ethnographic practices tended to ignore. The very least this implies is that theory and practice, a concept of culture and methods as well as agendas of research, are internally connected. This view is stated against positivist ideas postulating that data are given, methods exchangeable, and theories more or less arbitrary. Popular culture theory may have its most important task in helping to bring about (or complete) the demise of social scientific positivism. It complements in practice what the philosophical critique of the sixties and seventies argued in theory.

Another insight to be gained from work on and with popular culture is that the phenomenon—hence the problem—of power needs to be addressed on every conceivable level of conceptualization and analysis-interpretation. In situations like the ones I have looked at, those who produce and consume popular culture have been the victims of colonization and postcolonial oppression; for them popular culture has been a means of survival as well as a weapon of defense. But onslaught and resistance are not all there is to the struggle with and for power. There is "power within": before power is used or abused, its sources are constituted when popular culture emerges through the creation of generic forms (in chapter 2 I explored this by concentrating on genre). These forms give shape to products and expressions of popular culture; they also impose constraints on communication and artistic production. Genre, I showed, channels authority and creativity; it erects boundaries and thereby creates identities. By being negated (or at least negotiated), genre also makes innovation possible. The strength of popular culture derives from the fact that it is an ongoing process, that power is constantly established, negated, and reestablished. It is not its being power free that distinguishes popular culture from high or traditional culture, but its working against the accumulation and concentration of power, which, when institutionalized, cannot do without victims. Acts of creation and negation are the "moments of freedom" evoked in the title of this book. The challenge for the ethnographer, who is usually, and understandably, concerned with describing culture as something that lasts, is to catch popular culture when it is being energized. This will not be achieved by ethnographic routine; it takes moments of freedom to catch moments of freedom.

The terms "moment" and "catch" are metaphors of ethnography that signal the importance of temporality—of conceptions of time and practices of timing—in the study of popular culture to which I turned my attention in chapter 3. Observations on the privileging, in received culture theory, of shape over movement and of space over time made me consider the problem of contemporaneity as it poses itself specifically in the study of popular culture: as the coexistence of tradition and modernity. Such coexistence must be assumed and understood if our ambition is to recognize popular culture as contemporary practice, that is, as neither derivative epiphenomenon nor something that, in some evolutionary perspective on history, inevitably follows tradition when the latter disappears under the onslaught of modernity. There may be conceptual overlap between popular culture and ethnicity and globalization, but both of these approaches to contemporary Africa, I argued, are burdened with spatial categories and images that may get in the way of appreciating the temporality found essential in our understanding of popular culture.

Specifically, I considered the extraordinary demands that popular culture makes on the ethnographer when it comes to acknowledging its presence, hence its existence in the present, hence its copresence with practices of anthropological research. I dealt with this as "time respected." "Time contested" was the heading under which I examined evidence for ways with time in popular historiography. The principle of contemporaneity precludes relativizing, for instance, discrepancies of dating between popular accounts and academic chronology. Such discrepancies need to be understood as contesting official, academic knowledge as well as responding to performative necessities of timing characteristic of oral discourse.

African popular culture produces written and printed texts; however, it never ceases to speak with a live voice. That circumstance makes representing what we have experienced of African culture in its presence a problem for which the conventions of traditional ethnographic writing hold no solution. In sum, though we need to be conscious of temporality in all kinds of anthropological practice, the study of popular culture poses special challenges (and offers, as I also tried to show, special rewards).

From discussions of temporality as it is involved in conceptualization, experience, performance, and representations of popular culture, I returned in chapter 4 to questions of power and contestation. If contemporaneity is not a given, how is it achieved by African popular culture? Using the debate on democratization in Africa as a point of departure, I turned once again to research in Shaba, this time to probe expressions of popular culture for ways they can be said to give evidence of the capacity of African people to survive and, indeed, to overcome seemingly hopeless political marginalization and seemingly bottomless pauperization. Taking a clue from Ernest Wamba dia Wamba, a Zairian philosopher known for his critical position, I concentrated on popular thought about thinking, that is, on the motivation and capacity of Africans to master their present predicaments intellectually. In three contexts—song, religious teaching, and historiology—I followed the meaning of *kuwaza* and *mawazo,* thinking and thought. I discovered connections in popular thought between reflection and recall, thought and memory, that give thinking its practical and collective orientation. Not detached ratiocination, but reflection that draws on common experience is what keeps people going, makes them sing, proclaim their humanist visions of a good life, and give their realistic appraisal of history as it led to the present.

What I represented of popular culture in Zaire was selected to serve our theoretical discussion. I took care to make the ethnographic material I discussed come alive, and I hope that readers, even though they forget the arguments, will remember the examples. But the picture I painted was far from complete. As I promised in the preface, I should briefly indicate what I know is missing and what others may go on to explore in greater depth if and when research again becomes possible.

In my own work, I touched on popular literacy in the form of written history, but we need to know more about popular writing and reading in Shaba (including personal letters, memories and autobiographies, and dream books that we know exist but that are hard to come by). After I began writing these conclusions, I made an acquaintance that led me to change my view that in Zaire nothing existed that could be compared with, say, the Onitsha market literature in Nigeria described more than twenty years ago (Obiechina 1973). At a workshop on popular culture in Africa, I met Zamenga Batukezanga, a prolific writer of popular novels, tracts, and comic strips as well as a leader of projects for self-help in his native region on the border between Zaire and the Congo Republic. I am sure there are others like him in Zaire, even in Shaba, where I had never met a popular writer.

Storytelling, one of the strongest elements of tradition, is alive in urban culture as a kind of performance most adults and even children are expected to master with competence. Recent work in Lubumbashi has shown that the practice thrives in multilingual contexts (Gijsels 1996). Characteristically, it requires not only a repertory of tales, but also the ability to quote proverbs and sing songs (often in languages other than the common Swahili). There is evidence that classical themes and genres are transformed to suit present conditions (something that presumably has always occurred). My study of popular painting and historiography also revealed many direct links to storytelling. Still, much remains to be learned about how this practice relates to other expressions, especially with regard to how tradition and modernity relate in popular culture. And while we are on the topic of oral performances, I should at least mention that the history and characteristic structures of Shaba Swahili, the common medium of popular culture in this region, need to be further explored and documented. There are plans to do both by establishing archives of popular Swahili that will make accessible existing literature and textual documentation and provide a frame for work on relations between linguistic and cultural creolization. Aside from the dissertation by Gijsels already cited, there is another by Vincent de Rooij (1996) on code- and style-switching in Shaba. Here too much theoretical terrain remains to be explored. What is often presented as mixing or pastiche in expressions of popular culture may be illuminated by its linguistic counterparts.

It is, or was, a characteristic of popular culture in Zaire that it is not primarily a mass media culture, except for radio broadcasting, which became a major vehicle of popular music as well as of locally produced sketches and plays. Film and television were gaining importance, at least until the country fell into its present paralysis. Film had been introduced quite early (perhaps as early as the phonograph), first as an educational medium by the missions and by other colonial authorities, later also commercially. People in Shaba would eagerly attend showings, but I saw little evidence of a "movie world" in everyday life and talk. Quite to the contrary, the fledgling television I first encountered in Lubumbashi in the seventies was received by the population with great interest and much response. The sketches by the Mufwankolo troupe that were televised weekly were the talk of the town. They were discussed and retold and thus "consumed" by many more people than those who could actually watch them. In the eighties the televised Mufwankolo program became the victim of centralization and political control, made possible by a modernized, satellite-based broadcasting system set up in Kinshasa by French experts. In Lubumbashi in the mid-eighties, my impression was that local production and programming were at a rather low level and that television broadcasting was preempted by the popularity of video cassette rental in the middle class, both local and foreign.

Another interesting practice I was aware of, but could not really follow up on, was what one might call popular photography. I had indirect evidence that it was somehow in competition for space with popular painting and, at least in the seventies, it looked as if painting was winning, with the exception of portraits and commemorative family pictures. Bogumil Jewsiewicki is currently conducting research on this topic (see also several contributions to a recent special issue of *Cahiers d'Etudes Africaines*).

Sports (mainly soccer, but also bicycle racing in colonial times, company- or mission-sponsored athletic competitions, etc.) have been a major form of popular entertainment. Again my experiences were mainly indirect; sports were a frequent subject of conversation, and certain stars of the popular culture scene were also highly visible as supporters of soccer clubs (the singer Franco was behind a team in Kinshasa, the actress Balimuacha of the Mufwankolo troupe was president of a soccer fan club in Lubumbashi).

For a full picture of the history of popular culture one would also have to know more about drinking and smoking, the role of alcohol and tobacco as well as hemp. Drinking places were the sites of music, of dancing, but also of (mural) painting. They have been the meeting places of men and women who seek *ambiance,* the nearly untranslatable Zairian word for what one commentator has called a hedonistic culture (Biaya 1994). I must defer to Biaya, who speaks with the authority of someone who grew up in the culture he describes, but I have reservations regarding the general applicability of his interpretations and some of his historical reconstructions. Another fascinating recent development is the fusion of religion, men's fashion, and music in the *sapeur* movement led by pop star Papa Wemba (Friedman 1992; Gandoulou 1989).

Which, finally, brings us to another subject underrepresented in these essays: popular culture and gender. Women have been leaders in popular religion and stars in popular music. They have been arbiters of fashion in a culture where textiles and patterns are symbols of intricate distinction and the subject of much discussion. Why, when women are accomplished storytellers, actresses, and dancers, did I never encounter a female popular painter or writer? Gendered literacy, even in its grassroots forms, should be investigated. We encountered ideas and images of male-female relations when I discussed examples of religious and poetic discourse, but more needs to be known, for instance, about the role of the *femme libre,* an institution and social role that would be misunderstood if described, as it has sometimes been, simply as that of a prostitute (street prostitution and its more refined, but nevertheless strictly commercial, forms are a recent development in Zaire).

In sum, to the degree that the concept of popular culture has made us aware of many aspects of contemporary African life our traditional approaches tended to ignore, we are also discovering how much more we need to know, and present, in order to do justice to its vigor and complexity.

When I began taking stock of my research and ideas, I asked myself whether this book would become a manifesto or an epitaph for the concept of popular culture. As I look back on this project—and around at recent conferences and publications—I conclude that it is, or should be, both. It is a manifesto in that the conclusion can only be a plea for more attention to and better understanding of elements that, so far, seem to have been revealed mainly with the help of the concept of popular culture. It is an epitaph in that popular culture studies in Africa should probably be thought of as belonging to those self-liquidating disciplines, the need for which disappears to the extent that they are successful in accomplishing their work (sociolinguistics was once characterized as such by Dell Hymes, one of its inventors; who knows, anthropology itself may be another candidate).

The political vision behind popular culture as "moments of freedom" is decidedly not one of revolution and liberation, once and forever. In that sense it expresses disillusion; I share some of the leftist gloom, but certainly none of the rightist glee spread by the crash of oppressive regimes that called themselves socialist or Marxist. Of course, the end of oppression anywhere is a cause for joy; but is the victory of capitalism? What is Africa getting out of that victory? "Moments of freedom" do away with grand visions that have always depended on liberators: persons, doctrines, or political systems. That freedom comes in moments makes it impossible to distinguish, as a matter of uncontested principle, between societies that have it and others that do not. Commitment to such an idea (no matter how many rational choices or expedient compromises one makes when preferring to live in one society or state rather than another) requires thought capable of transcending received distinctions. Such thought may have to be more radical than the ideas that have moved either the missionaries of democracy or the prophets of revolution. By inventing all those things and practices we call popular culture, its creators may be so much ahead of us intellectuals in understanding the current state of the world that we could get discouraged—if it weren't that every one of us can, somehow and to some extent, join the talk, see the images, dance to the music, and remember the stories.

✧ ✧ ✧

Notes

1. Popular Culture in Anthropology

1. Though it should be obvious by now, it may still be useful to point out that, in spite of the linguistic form (noun + adjective), culture and popular culture are not related logically as general and specific terms or as class and member. Popular culture is not in the same class of concepts as, say, musical culture, medieval culture, or French culture. If anything, its logical status (not its content) resembles that of "primitive culture."

2. I am quoting from memory a remark to the seventh Jahnheinz Jahn Symposium (Mainz, 10–11 November 1995) by Mantuba Mabiala of the University of Kinshasa. His statement was enthusiastically supported by another participant from Zaire, Zamenga Batukezanga, a popular writer from that country.

3. Most recently this approach, the Harvard and Chicago paradigm, has been described by Clifford Geertz (1995). Sherry Ortner, a classmate of mine at Chicago, reported a decade ago what became of anthropological culture theory in the eighties (1984). For an attempt to assess the concept of culture at the present time see Brightman 1995.

4. See the locus classicus in Franz Boas's introduction to the *Handbook of American Indian Languages* (1911). George Stocking has traced the development toward a plural conception (1968 and many later publications). For a recent critique of "fundamentalist" uses of culture see Stolcke 1995.

5. The project was initially supported by grant RO-6150-72-149 from the U.S. National Endowment for the Humanities.

6. An exception was Epstein's colleague and mentor Clyde Mitchell, whose study of the Kalela dance (1956) must count as one of the most remarkable studies of an element of African popular culture *avant la lettre*. Also in this tradition was Terence O. Ranger's pioneering study on dance and society in East Africa (1975). For an important postcolonial appraisal of life in Zambia during colonial times see the essays edited by Samuel N. Chipungu (1992), especially the chapter on "popular culture in a colonial society" by Albert B. K. Matongo.

7. Notably that of Ulf Hannerz (1987; on his current views see Hannerz 1992). For a critique of the (over)use of creolization see Parkin 1993.

8. The result was an essay titled "Time and the Other: How Anthropology Makes Its Object." I completed a first draft in 1978; it took another five years before, after several rejections, it appeared in print (Fabian 1983).

9. In two papers published with my former wife and coresearcher: Szombati-Fabian and Fabian 1976 and Fabian and Szombati-Fabian 1980.

10. This brief account has mainly British and American work in mind; in contrast, see the considerable influence of the pioneering work of Georges Balandier (1955, 1957) and one of the first general critiques of African studies by Gérard Leclerc (1971).

11. Jan Vansina's *De la tradition orale* (1961) appeared in an English translation in 1965. Twenty years later he radically revised his classic (1985). For a detailed history of "African history" see the same author's recent recollections (1994).

12. Another genre of which at least a few examples have surfaced is the more individually oriented life history. Unfortunately we can do little more than guess the importance of such productions of popular literacy. Their form alone made it unlikely that they would have appeared in any of the printed media that existed during colonial times.

13. I vividly recall reading this remarkable exchange, but unfortunately I must report it from memory. At the time I took a reference and excerpted the newspaper items, but I somehow lost the file. At the moment I have no access to the specialized library where I found copies of the short-lived newspaper (probably in the collection kept at the Benedictine Abbey of St. Andrew near Bruges). I do remember that the scribe in question was said to have been of West African origin. West Africans, together with the so-called Nyasaland boys, educated workers and clerks from what is now Malawi, carried literacy to the Congo outside the channels controlled mostly by the missions. Since it is not likely that literacy was passed on as a mere tool, we may assume that it also transmitted to the Congo urban experiences made by other Africans in their home countries. Just how permeable colonial boundaries were from the beginning for the creations of popular culture deserves to be studied more fully.

14. It is useful to remember at this point that interest in the "nitty-gritty" details of daily life inspired an ethnographic turn in historiography

and that the notion of popular culture played a crucial role in that reorientation. Work associated with the names of Carlo Ginsburg (1976) and Peter Burke (1978), among others, comes to mind. I remember that when I started out to work on popular art in Shaba I was most impressed by Michael Baxandall's study of Italian Renaissance painting (1972), a view I shared with Clifford Geertz, who drew on Baxandall for his essay "Art as a Cultural System" (in Geertz 1983).

15. For anthropological discussions of art and culture see the essay by Geertz mentioned earlier (note 14) and especially James Clifford's critical observations (1988, index).

16. I found this confirmed in Goody's appraisal in *The Expansive Moment: Anthropology in Britain and Africa, 1918–1970* (1995). Popular culture is not an entry in the index; culture contact is, but in almost all instances it refers to remarks about its being a topic that was forced on British anthropologists by one of their major sponsors, the Rockefeller Foundation. Urban anthropology is mentioned in passing. In the chapter summarizing "achievements of anthropology in Africa," Goody states: "There was relatively little work carried out on social change since it was felt that priority should be given to indigenous societies . . . only with independence did serious academic research pay much attention to the changing situation. So the directions laid down by the Rockefeller philanthropies had surprisingly little influence on what research was actually carried out and written up" (1995, 115–16). Powdermaker 1962 was a notable exception.

17. The study of African popular arts was surveyed with admirable thoroughness by Karin Barber (1987; see also a similar survey of research in performance in Africa by Margaret Thompson Drewal 1991). Barber (1997) is currently also assembling a reader of essays on the theory of popular culture in Africa.

18. Approaching religious independence in the colonized world as "religions of the oppressed" had the considerable merit of establishing the political significance of "reaction" in a religious idiom (the classic study is Lanternari 1963). It had its limitations when it came to accounting for the specific cultural content that made such reaction creative.

19. See note 4 above.

20. Of course, colonials would have had an answer ready: the joke was in the inappropriate, ill-understood use of Western culture. But that expla-

nation begs the question of who decides what is appropriate and well understood. There is a lesson in this, though: we should take seriously whatever strikes us as funny when we study popular culture.

21. See also a collection of essays in honor of Victor Turner assembled around the theme of creativity (Lavie, Narayan, and Rosaldo 1993).

22. On mimesis and alterity see also Taussig 1993.

23. I will return to this dilemma in the next chapter. For an attempt to examine solutions, and escapes, see Fabian 1991, chap. 13.

24. It is, of course, tempting to address similar reflections to sociology, psychology, and closer to home, human evolution, prehistory, and archaeology. Twenty-five years ago Alvin Gouldner began his sweeping critique of "Western sociology" with observations on "sociology as popular culture." Notice, however, that this was directed against "the mass availability" of "paperback sociology of the bookstore" and that he considered this mingling of sociology with "other expressions of popular literature" something to be deplored (1970, 4).

25. The hypothesis I am advancing is of interest only to the extent that it helps us recognize specific reasons why a discourse on popular culture could and should include anthropology among its subjects. On some level, everything is of course connected to everything, but that is not what I am asserting here.

26. An example would be an idea, formulated twenty-five years ago, that led to the collection of essays titled *Beyond Charisma: Religious Movements as Discourse* (Fabian 1979a). It started with the realization that anthropologists and prophets find themselves facing similar tasks. It now can be argued that the future challenge will be to do research and write ethnographies *with,* not just *of,* the people we study (see Fabian 1991b, 5–6).

27. Probably I should be more cautious and ask, "What took this anthropologist so long?" That others had come to similar positions is quite likely. Also, I should check my notes and earlier publications. Still, as far as I can recall, likely candidates for forerunners such as Melville Herskovits and some of his students who had begun to think of contemporary African culture on both sides of the Atlantic had not been moved to a serious challenge of the tenets of culturalism.

28. Of course, how old that debate is may itself be debated. Serious attempts to document the full range of "popular arts," and to explore their nature, go back quite some time, arguably to the classic essay of 1893 by

Alois Riegl (1978), for instance, and to an international congress on that topic held in 1928 at Prague, sponsored by the League of Nations. Henri Focillon's introduction to the published proceedings (1931) documents a resolve to salvage, as it were, popular arts from a narrow "folkloric" vision. Focillon sketches a notion of popular culture as contemporary ("L'histoire est faite des plus de communications que de conservations," xi). Compared with this, the basically anthropological concept of culture—evolutionary and scientific—as it was adopted by UNESCO after World War II looks rather regressive (see Huxley 1949). Incidentally, the Prague volume also contained a contribution titled "L'art chez les populations indigènes du Congo Belge" by E. de Jonghe, a truly remarkable inclusion given the prevalent opposition of popular and primitive art. I thank Nina Gorgus and Tamás Hofer for bringing the Prague congress to my attention.

29. For instance, popular culture as a discursive practice dictated by what she calls "dominant culture" (Shiach 1989, 6–7, 21–22); the motif of the student of culture being always "just a little too late" (12); the popular as "the other" (31); the "timelessness" that often characterizes popular culture studies (29).

30. There is an aside to her observation: by now it is generally accepted that the study of material culture, especially as it regards commodification and (mass) consumption, is an important aspect of the study of popular culture (see, for instance, Miller 1987). Within living memory—my own—material culture was considered a marginal, hence largely female, domain.

31. See Shiach 1989, 16–17; Rowe and Schelling 1991, 9–10 and throughout. Gramsci does not appear in these essays because I cannot claim that I came to my findings (or for that matter my questions) through studying his thought. If there are convergences they must be due to similar historical and practical contexts. The same goes, more or less, for obligatory references to, say, Bakhtin and Foucault (although I spelled out what I learned from the latter in my 1978 essay).

32. This list is, with minute changes, repeated twice in the second chapter (Scott 1985, 29, 34) and, in a version that is in my view much improved, it concludes the book when we are invited to see "tenacity of self-preservation . . . in ridicule, in truculence, in irony, in petty acts of non-compliance, in foot dragging, in resistant mutuality, in the disbelief in elite homilies, in the steady, grinding efforts to hold one's own against overwhelming odds" (350).

2. Power Within

1. What goes for genre goes for rule concepts in general. For a discussion of rules and power in linguistics, a field whose very existence has been linked to high and low distinctions, see Joseph and Taylor 1990. For an empirical study of genre and power in disciplinary training and communication, see Berkenkotter and Huckin 1995.

2. This has been done recently by many literary critics, and most closely related to our concerns, by Edward Said in his *Culture and Imperialism* (1993).

3. A collection of essays on genre in folklore studies and anthropology, including his own landmark paper "Analytical Categories and Ethnic Genres," was edited by Dan Ben-Amos (1976). For a survey of the current situation—and an example of the struggle with the dilemmas the concept creates—see Finnegan 1992, chap. 7; also Briggs and Bauman 1992. Jan Vansina's thorough revision of his earlier work on oral tradition should be mentioned (1985). How perceptive and interesting anthropological work on genre has gotten recently is demonstrated by Elizabeth Tonkin in her book on the "social construction of oral history" (1992; see esp. chaps. 2 and 3).

4. For ethnographic detail I must refer to published sources: De Craemer 1977; Fabian 1971, 1991.

5. For references to the history of publication and reception of this book see chapter 4 below, where I will discuss some of Tempels's ideas in more detail.

6. I will have more to say about this in chapter 4. Perhaps this is the moment to recall that the presentation of ethnography in these essays is neither monographic nor systematic. I work with repeated starts, depending on the theoretical issue I want to raise; therefore some repetition is inevitable.

7. See also the remarks at the end of chapter 1.

8. Because at the time I was as yet little aware of the performance aspects of communication, I omitted prayer and communal singing from my list: the former, unlike the other genres, did not seem distinctive of the movement; in the latter case I felt unable to deal with the technicalities of musical performance.

9. Physically the closest were the Zairean followers of John Maranke,

called Bapostolo and studied by Bennetta Jules-Rosette (1975). The most important contribution of her book was that she, literally, followed the movement of the Bapostolo between the Kasai region and what was then still Southern Rhodesia. For a long time, that movements moved was just about the last thing sociologists would consider when studying their organization and ideology.

10. There were also connections, still to be explored and documented in detail, to the Catholic *cursillo* movement in Europe and the United States (Marcoux 1982). The *cursillo,* in turn, contributed to the emergence of the "multinational" Catholic charismatic, neo-Pentecostal movement (Csordas 1980, most recently 1994) which, to close this particular circle of global circulation of ideas and practices, came to challenge the Jamaa movement in the seventies (see chapter 4).

11. For this see Szombati-Fabian and Fabian 1976 and Fabian 1996.

12. I have been using the past tense here and elsewhere in talking about popular painting in Shaba. Although comparable practices that emerged in other parts of Zaire (and, of course, elsewhere in Africa and the Third World) seem to be alive, for instance, in Kinshasa and in the north of the country (see Jewsiewicki 1991), production came to a halt in Shaba sometime in the late seventies. The political troubles of that time (the "Shaba invasions" of 1976 and 1978) may be to blame, but the decisive factor was that pauperization had reached a level that made buying a painting a luxury people could no longer afford.

13. As I noted earlier, in the seventies I discovered Shaba genre painting through pictures displayed in the houses of Jamaa followers, including one genre (the mermaid) that seemed to conflict with a Christian religious orientation but had a crucial significance within the system of genres of memory. Later I found that Jamaa followers used genre painting much the same way as other members of the population.

14. See my proposal to extend the communication model toward ethnography as performance (Fabian 1990b).

15. This qualification is important. First, I did hear several Jamaa leaders with a pedagogical bent or background delivering their instructions (*mafundisho*) in a question-response format. But that was a stylistic choice that was permitted within the genre; it was no more conversational than a catechism (which may have been the model). Second, one of the traits of popular speech that also showed up in Jamaa teaching is antiphonal ex-

change (call and response) between a speaker and his or her audience. Such exchanges may involve responding to questions; most frequently they consist of completing words or phrases that are prompted by the speaker with the help of a particular intonation pattern. The result is often a rhythmic back-and-forth, a dialogue between speaker and audience that is purely performative.

16. On Desfossés see the brief remarks and a few illustrations in Fabian and Szombati-Fabian 1980, 280–85.

17. See also the remarks on metaphorically disguised comments on the colonial situation in popular song texts (chapter 4).

18. It also invites comparison with remarkably similar developments elsewhere (for instance in Haiti and Nigeria). One of the most conspicuous "schools" of painting emerged in Bali. Hildred Geertz has embarked on a thorough and perceptive study of this institution. A first volume (1995) focuses on the collection of Balinese paintings assembled by Margaret Mead and Gregory Bateson.

19. One of the major reasons for employing the concept of popular culture is that it does not require us to postulate unity or uniformity. Still, my views of popular culture have come under suspicion of populism (Geschiere 1995, reacting to a short keynote address of which parts were incorporated in chapter 1 above). What else can an anthropologist do, unless we delude ourselves by thinking of our work as never taking sides? At the same time, populism and popular culture should be kept conceptually apart. I try to show that in certain instances and situations popular culture may work against the people.

20. I dealt with this in an essay titled "Text and Terror" (Fabian 1979c; reprinted in Fabian 1991, chap. 4).

21. See an early comprehensive study by Greschat (1967), followed by Gerard (1969, with a focus on Zaire and based on original documents) and an interesting case study on Kitawala among Kumu (Komo) mineworkers by Mwene-Batende (1982). The Watch Tower movement also has an important place in Karen Fields's study of religious resistance to colonial rule (1985). These references are only a few examples; on the whole, our knowledge of Kitawala remains fragmentary and "screened" by successive regimes of oppression. A hypothesis I would like to see explored is that, by using Swahili as spoken in Katanga shortly after World War I, Kitawala pioneered popular religious discourse in that language.

22. This, incidentally, leads one to suspect that much of the practice of folklore collecting that may have understood itself as preserving authentic traditions, and is as such generally contrasted with popular culture, has in fact been part of the construction of popular culture.

23. At about the same time Europeans mounted what was called *spectacles populaires,* multigenre performances of ethnic dances against backdrops painted by, among others, the young Mwenze of the Desfossés school. In scale and intent, these were colonial celebrations of Congolese folklore that had little or no influence on the rise of popular theater (see Fabian 1990b, 49–50).

24. Erlmann takes an approach linking performance and power in his study of a form of South African popular music, Isicathamiya (1996). Perhaps even more than in Zairian popular music, creators and performers are driven by competition.

3. Time and Movement in Popular Culture

1. Other anthropologists have been led to similar positions along different routes; see especially Augé 1994.

2. See, for instance, Turner 1993 for "Luba," "Tetela," and "Basonge"; see Roberts 1984 for "Tabwa."

3. After World War II, when recording got seriously under way, small entrepreneurs (often Greek) maintained studios in several of the larger cities. As international companies began to take an interest in the African market, the "industry"—and therefore also the "scene"—concentrated on Léopoldville-Kinshasa (Bemba 1984; Bender 1991a; Ewens 1991, 1994). Some of the pioneers of popular music in Katanga-Shaba (Low 1982) who sang in Swahili found a market in East Africa, at least for a while. One of the greatest artists, Jean-Bosco Mwenda, never abandoned Swahili and became increasingly marginalized from the modern scene (more about Jean Bosco in the following chapter).

4. Biaya (1988) seems to argue that ethnicity informs recent popular painting in Zaire. He shows that it is a *topic* (How could commentators on everyday reality avoid it?) but offers nothing that suggests differentiation of styles or genres along ethnic lines. His real concern in this paper is not to explain ethnicity but to blame it for what he perceives as magical, nonrational elements in contemporary painting.

5. They may be found in writings ranging from ethnographic papers now considered classics (Evans-Pritchard 1939) to broad statements such as those by theologian-philosopher John Mbiti (1990, critically discussed most recently by Masolo 1994, chap. 5). More directly relevant to the discussion that follows is recent work on temporality in the "social construction of oral history" (see Tonkin 1992, chap. 4). For the wider ethnographic and theoretical background consult the comprehensive overview of anthropological approaches to time in Munn 1992. Articles and books on the topic have continued to appear in recent years.

6. The term "historiology" was proposed by Jan Vansina, the foremost methodologist of "oral tradition as history" (1985). It is intended to overcome the graphic bias in concepts such as historiography and to undermine the long-established opposition between oral and written history.

7. In thinking about differences between mere chronicling and historical narration, I have been inspired by an often-cited essay by Hayden White (1980; for an application to popular historiology see Fabian 1990a, 190–93).

8. Technological developments now make it possible to combine written accounts with visual and acoustic recordings of events (with the help of CD-ROMs; see Keersenboom 1995). They open up new dimensions, but I suspect that they multiply challenges rather than provide solutions to the problems of ethnographic representation.

9. See, for instance, Bal 1993, 311, and Harding 1993.

4. African Presence

1. On African images see, among others, two books commenting on exhibitions, Boly 1985 and Nederveen-Pieterse 1992. Of interest are also early projects aimed at revealing Africa through its graphic images (Leyder 1947; Macquet-Tombu 1947; Mortier 1947; Périer 1947; Périer and Leyder 1947–48).

2. See the essays on *Présence Africaine,* the journal and the idea, edited by Mudimbe (1992).

3. Nevertheless, some kinds of presence are more curious than others: A sample of work by Chéri Samba, reproduced in color, inscriptions on paintings translated into English (by Bogumil Jewsiewicki) appeared in a

magazine for what look like hard-core cartoon addicts: *Raw: High Culture for Low Brows* 3–4 (1991): 12–19 (published by Penguin). On Chéri Samba see also Jewsiewicki 1995. While writing this chapter, I happened to see on Dutch television images, unmistakably either partial copies of paintings by Mode Muntu or otherwise lifted from them, being projected in flashes on the walls of a technodisco in Amsterdam.

4. Transcribed from a tape made in the mid-eighties. The last morpheme, *bo,* I take to be a filler. On Jean-Bosco Mwenda and the development of distinctive guitar styles in Shaba see Low 1982. I knew Mwenda personally and heard him perform several times within a small circle of friends. Although marginalized by the eventual establishment of the music industry in Kinshasa, Jean-Bosco Mwenda had made appearances and was widely known in Europe and America.

5. See on this Ewens's biography of Franco (1994). Male-female relations and representations of gender in Zairean popular music are the topic of Ph.D. research being done by Walu Engundu under my direction.

6. For a comprehensive statement of that position see my survey of the anthropology of religious movements (Fabian 1979b), which, as the genre demands, was fairly conservative. Compare this with a paper that appeared in the same year and another general essay two years later (Fabian 1979d, 1981, reprinted in Fabian 1991, chap. 6). Both were informed by the change of perspective that came with the discovery of popular culture (1978). One of the theses I formulated in the 1981 piece was: "The surrogate-tribe and answer-to-the-colonial-situation views of African religious movements were rooted in a concept of culture which may no longer be appropriate. An alternative could be to see in religious movements expressions of an emerging popular culture" (1991, 121).

7. See the writings of Georges Balandier, notably 1955, 1957.

8. On the "ethnophilosophical" significance of Tempels, and on ethnophilosophy as a discourse, see Mudimbe 1988; Appiah 1992; and Masolo 1994. These works, and also the anthology edited by Smet (1975), may be consulted for other references. As far as I know, none of the philosophical appreciations and critiques of *Bantu Philosophy* has so far accepted my argument that Tempels cannot be understood except in the full historical context of his work, which includes the Jamaa movement (Fabian 1970, revised and reprinted in Smet 1975, 2:383–409). This, I believe, is symp-

tomatic of the fixation of ethnophilosophers on supposedly authentic traditions and a general disdain for supposedly inauthentic contemporary popular culture.

9. Distancing and contestation required acknowledgment of a common ground: *kazi,* work, became a quasi-cosmological concept in Jamaa teaching (Fabian 1973).

10. Even to begin to document this with bibliographical references would take us too far away. I shall mention just a few titles: a collection of the writings of Archbishop Milingo (1984), leader of the charismatics in neighboring Zambia; a study focused on the bishop's work by Gerrie Ter Haar (1992); and a general appraisal of the Charismatic Renewal in a collection of essays edited by Karla Poewe (1994).

11. For an informative attempt to assess the role of Christian denominations in the opposition to the Mobutu regime during the early years of this decade see Kabongo-Mbaya 1994; see also René Devisch's valiant effort to make sense of chaos in Kinshasa (1995).

12. More than intimations: names and cases of prominent converts, including one of the regime's most notorious henchmen.

13. On *savoirs* see Chabal 1986 and Jewsiewicki and Moniot 1988.

14. As I noted before, I use this term following a suggestion made by Jan Vansina (1986, 109).

15. Benoît Verhaegen (1974), advocating an approach he called *histoire immédiate,* pioneered inquiries into popular history in Zaire; see also a collection of homages to Verhaegen (Omasombo 1993). Much of the recent work of Bogumil Jewsiewicki could be cited here (especially 1993), as well as an overview of forms of resistance in the colonial history of Zaire by Jan-Luc Vellut (1987).

16. See Fabian 1996. For more information on aspects of Tshibumba's work see also Jewsiewicki (for instance, 1991 and the collection of essays he edited in 1992).

17. One should be wary of spatial metaphors, yet some are nevertheless useful. In this case the notion of a terrain helps us envisage the establishment of practices we can return to as to a familiar place and, more important, lets us posit a concrete common ground for contestation, an element that is often left abstract and general in impact-and-resistance models of colonialism.

18. I hesitate, therefore, to accept Mudimbe's suggestion (derived from

Fabian 1969) that *gnosis* may be one way of characterizing generally what has been called "African philosophy" (1988, ix).

19. Parts of this chapter incorporate a contribution to a panel called "Contested Terrain: Democratization at the Local Level in Africa," sponsored by SSRC and CODESRIA and organized by Catharine Newbury for the thirty-sixth annual meeting of the African Studies Association, Boston, 4–7 December 1993. For the agenda of that discussion and its orientation see Newbury's introduction (1994) and other contributions to a special issue of *African Studies Review*. See also a recent overview and bibliography on democratization in Africa compiled in the Netherlands (Buijtenhuijs and Rijnerse 1993).

20. And, I may add, when we consider the implications of Tshibumba's report on the absence of organization among artists quoted in the second fragment above, in popular culture. Ewens's biography of Franco (1994) adds much confirming evidence from the history of popular music.

21. Perhaps it takes anarchists to recognize the significance of anarchy in contemporary Africa. A remarkable study, or rather collage, that came to my attention too late to be commented on in these essays is the book by David Hecht and Maliqualim Simone (1994).

✧ ✧ ✧

References

Appiah, Anthony Kwame. 1992. *In My Father's House: Africa in the Philosophy of Culture.* New York: Oxford Univ. Press.

Asch, Susan. 1983. *L'église du prophète Kimbangu: Des ses origines à son role actuel au Zaïre.* Paris: Karthala.

Augé, Marc. 1994. *Pour une anthropologie des mondes contemporains.* Paris: Aubier.

Bal, Mieke. 1993. "First Person, Second Person, Same Person: Narrative as Epistemology." *New Literary History* 24:293–320.

Balandier, Georges. 1955. *Sociologie actuelle de l'Afrique noire.* Paris: Presses Universitaires de France.

———. 1957. *Afrique ambigüe.* Paris: Plon.

Barber, Karin. 1987. "Popular Arts in Africa." *African Studies Review* 30 (3): 1–78.

———, ed. 1997. *Readings in African Popular Culture.* Bloomington: Indiana Univ. Press.

Bauman, Richard, et al. 1977. *Verbal Art as Performance.* 2d ed. Prospect Heights IL: Waveland Press.

———. 1986. *Story, Performance and Event: Contextual Studies of Oral Narrative.* Cambridge: Cambridge Univ. Press.

Bauman, Zygmunt. 1973. *Culture as Praxis.* London: Routledge & Kegan Paul.

Bausinger, Hermann. 1986. *Volkskultur in der technischen Welt.* Stuttgart: Kohlhammer, 1961. Reprint Frankfurt: Campus.

Baxandall, Michael. 1972. *Painting and Experience in Fifteenth Century Italy.* London: Oxford Univ. Press.

Bayart, Jean-François. 1989. *L'état en Afrique: La politique du ventre.* Paris: Fayard.

———. 1993. *The State in Africa: The Politics of the Belly.* London: Longman.

Bemba, Sylvain. 1984. *50 ans de musique du Congo-Zaire.* Paris: Présence Africaine.

Ben-Amos, Dan, ed. 1976. *Folkore Genres.* Austin: Univ. of Texas Press.

Bender, Wolfgang, ed. 1991a. *Chéri Samba.* Munich: Trickster.

———. 1991b. *Sweet Mother: Modern African Music.* Chicago: Univ. of Chicago Press.

Berger, Arthur Asa. 1992. *Popular Culture Genres: Theories and Texts.* Newbury Park CA: Sage.

Berkenkotter, Carol, and Thomas N. Huckin. 1995. *Genre Knowledge in Disciplinary Communication: Cognition/Power/Culture.* Hillsdale NJ: Erlbaum.

Biaya, T. K. 1988. "L'impasse de la crise zairoise dans la peinture populaire urbaine, 1970–1985." *Canadian Journal of African Studies* 22:95–120.

———. 1994. "*Ndumba, mundele* et *ambiance:* Le vrai 'Bal blanc et noir(e).'" In *Belgique/Zaire: Une histoire en quête d'avenir,* ed. Gauthier de Villers, 85–100. Brussels: CEDAF; Paris: Harmattan.

Boas, Franz. 1911. Introduction to *Handbook of American Indian Languages.* Washington DC: Government Printing Office.

Boly, J., ed. 1985. *Zaire, 1885–1985: Cent ans de regards belges.* Brussels: Coopération par l'Education et la Culture (CEC).

Briggs, Charles, and Richard Bauman. 1992. "Genre, Intertextuality, and Social Power." *Journal of Linguistic Anthropology* 2 (2): 131–72.

Brightman, Robert. 1995. "Forget Culture: Replacement, Transcendence, Relexification." *Cultural Anthropology* 10:509–46.

Brockmann, Rolf, and Gerd Hötter. 1994. *Szene Lagos: Reise in eine afrikanische Kultur-Metropole.* Munich: Trickster.

Buijtenhuijs, Rob, and Elly Rijnerse. 1993. *Democratization in Sub-Saharan Africa (1989–1992): An Overview of the Literature.* Leiden: African Studies Centre.

Burke, Peter. 1978. *Popular Culture in Early Modern Europe.* London: Oxford Univ. Press.

Cahiers d'Etudes Africaines. 1996. Special issue on "Images," 36 (1–2).

Certeau, Michel de. 1984. *The Practice of Everyday Life.* Berkeley: Univ. of California Press.

Chabal, P., ed. 1986. *Political Domination in Africa: Reflections on the Limits of Power.* Cambridge: Cambridge Univ. Press.

Chipungu, Samuel N., ed. 1992. *Guardians of Their Time: Experiences of Zambians under Colonial Rule, 1890–1964.* London: Macmillan.

Clarke, John, Chas Critcher, and Richard Johnson, eds. 1979. *Working Class Culture: Studies in History and Theory.* London: Hutchinson.

Clifford, James. 1988. *The Predicament of Culture:. Twentieth-Century Ethnography, Literature, and Art.* Cambridge: Harvard Univ. Press.
Clifford, James, and George E. Marcus, eds. 1986. *Writing Culture:. The Poetics and Politics of Ethnography.* Berkeley: Univ. of California Press.
Cosentino, Donald J. 1992. "Review of J. Fabian, *Power and Performance.*" *Research in African Literatures* 23:114–17.
Csáky, Moritz. 1996. *Ideologie der Operette und Wiener Moderne: Ein kulturhistorischer Essay zur österreichischen Identität.* Vienna: Böhlau.
Csordas [Chordas], Thomas J. 1980. "Building the Kingdom: The Creativity of Ritual Performance in Catholic Pentecostalism." Ph.D. diss., Department of Anthropology, Duke University.
———. 1994. *The Sacred Self: A Cultural Phenomenology of Charismatic Healing.* Berkeley: Univ. of California Press.
De Craemer, Willy. 1977. *The Jamaa and the Church: A Bantu Catholic Movement in Zaire.* Oxford: Clarendon.
Devisch, René. 1995. "Frenzy, Violence, and Ethical Renewal in Kinshasa." *Public Culture* 7:593–629.
Epstein, A. L. 1992. *Scenes from African Urban Life: Collected Copperbelt Essays.* Aberdeen: Edinburgh Univ. Press.
Erlmann, Veit. 1996. *Nightsong: Performance, Power, and Practice in South Africa.* Chicago: Univ. of Chicago Press.
Evans-Pritchard, E. E. 1939. "Nuer Time Reckoning." *Africa* 12:189–216.
Ewens, Graeme. 1991. *Africa O-Yé: A Celebration of African Music.* Enfield: Guinness.
———. 1994. *Congo Colossus: The Life and Legacy of Franco and OK Jazz.* Norfolk: Buku Press.
Fabian, Johannes. 1966. "Dream and Charisma: 'Theories of Dreams' in the Jamaa Movement (Congo)." *Anthropos* 61:544–60.
———. 1969. "An African Gnosis: For a Reconsideration of an Authoritative Definition." *History of Religions* 9:42–58.
———. 1970. *Philosophie Bantoue: Placide Tempels et son oeuvre vus dans une perspective historique.* Brussels: Centre de Recherche et d'Information Socio-politiques.
———. 1971. *Jamaa: A Charismatic Movement in Katanga.* Evanston IL: Northwestern Univ. Press.
———. 1973. "*Kazi:* Conceptualizations of Labor in a Charismatic Move-

ment among Swahili-Speaking Workers." *Cahiers d'Etudes Africaines* 13: 293–325.

———. 1974. "Genres in an Emerging Tradition: An Approach to Religious Communication." In *Changing Perspectives in the Scientific Study of Religion,* ed. A. W. Eister, 249–72. New York: Wiley Interscience.

———. 1977. Lore and Doctrine: Some Observations on Story-Telling in the Jamaa Movement. *Cahiers d'Etudes Africaines* 17:307–29.

———. 1978. "Popular Culture in Africa: Findings and Conjectures." *Africa* 48:315–34.

———, ed. 1979a. "Beyond Charisma: Religious Movements as Discourse." Special issue of *Social Research* 46 (1).

———. 1979b. "The Anthropology of Religious Movements: From Explanation to Interpretation." In "Beyond Charisma: Religious Movements as Discourse," ed. Johannes Fabian. Special issue of *Social Research* 46 (1): 4–35.

———. 1979c. "Text as Terror: Second Thoughts on Charisma." In "Beyond Charisma: Religious Movements as Discourse," ed. Johannes Fabian. Special issue of *Social Research* 46 (1): 166–203.

———. 1979d. "Man and Woman in the Teachings of the Jamaa Movement." In *The New Religions of Africa,* ed. Bennetta Jules-Rosette, 169–83. Norwood NJ: Ablex.

———. 1981. "Six Theses regarding the Anthropology of African Religious Movements." *Religion* 11:109–26.

———. 1983. *Time and the Other: How Anthropology Makes Its Object.* New York: Columbia Univ. Press.

———. 1986. *Language and Colonial Power:. The Appropriation of Swahili in the Former Belgian Congo, 1880–1938.* Cambridge: Cambridge Univ. Press. Reprint Berkeley: Univ. of California Press, 1991.

———. 1990a. *History from Below: The "Vocabulary of Elisabethville" by André Yav.* Philadelphia: John Benjamins.

———. 1990b. *Power and Performance: Ethnographic Exploration through Proverbial Wisdom and Theater in Shaba, Zaire.* Madison: Univ. of Wisconsin Press.

———. 1991. *Time and the Work of Anthropology: Critical Essays 1971–1991.* Chur, Switzerland: Harwood Academic.

———. 1994. "Jamaa: A Charismatic Movement Revisited." In *Religion in Africa: Experience and Expression,* ed. Thomas D. Blakely, Walter E. A.

van Beek, and Dennis L. Thomson, 257–74. London: James Currey; Portsmouth NH: Heineman.

———. 1996. *Remembering the Present: Painting and Popular History in Zaire.* Berkeley: Univ. of California Press.

Fabian, Johannes, and Ilona Szombati-Fabian. 1980. "Folk Art from an Anthropological Perspective." In *Perspectives on American Folk Art,* ed. Ian M. Quimby and Scott T. Swank, 247–92. New York: Norton.

Fetter, Bruce. 1974. "African Associations in Elisabethville, 1910–1930: Their Origins and Development." *Etudes d'Histoire Africaine* 4: 206–10.

———. 1976. *The Creation of Elisabethville: 1910–1940.* Stanford CA: Hoover Institution Press.

Fields, Karen E. 1985. *Revival and Rebellion in Colonial Central Africa.* Princeton: Princeton Univ. Press.

Finnegan, Ruth. 1992. *Oral Traditions and the Verbal Arts: A Guide to Research Practices.* London: Routledge.

Fiske, John. 1991. *Understanding Popular Culture.* London: Routledge.

Focillon, Henri. 1931. "Introduction." In Institut International de Coopération Intellectuelle, *International Congress of Popular Arts, Prague, October 7–13, 1928,* 1:vii–xvi. 2 vols. Paris: Éditions Duchartre.

Friedman, Jonathan. 1992. "The Political Economy of Elegance." *Culture and History* 7: 101–25.

Frobenius, Leo. 1928. *Das sterbende Afrika: Die Seele eines Erdteils.* Frankfurt am Main: Frankfurter Societäts-Druckerei.

Gandoulou, Justin-Daniel. 1989. *Dandies à Bacongo: Le culte d'élégance dans la société congolaise contemporaine.* Paris: Harmattan.

Geertz, Clifford. 1973. *The Interpretation of Cultures.* New York: Basic Books.

———. 1983. *Local Knowledge: Further Essays on Interpretive Anthropology.* New York: Basic Books.

———. 1995. *After the Fact: Two Countries, Four Decades, One Anthropologist.* Cambridge: Harvard Univ. Press.

Geertz, Hildred. 1995. *Images of Power: Balinese Paintings Made for Gregory Bateson and Margaret Mead.* Honolulu: Univ. of Hawaii Press.

Gerard, J. E. 1969. *Les fondements syncrétiques du Kitawala.* Brussels: CRISP.

Geschiere, Peter. 1995. "Populism, Old and New: Provisional Notes on the Concept 'Popular' in African Studies." In *Popular Culture: Africa, Asia, and Europe,* ed. J. van der Klei, 41–50. Proceedings Summer School CERES/CNWS 1994. Utrecht: CERES/CNWS.

Gijsels, Marjolein. 1996. "Genre, Intertextualiteit en Performance: Een etnographische studie van de hadisi. Een orale traditie in Lubumbashi, Zaire." Ph.D. diss., University of Amsterdam: Department of Anthropology.

Ginsburg, Carlo. 1976. *The Cheese and the Worms*. Baltimore: Johns Hopkins Univ. Press.

Goody, Jack. 1995. *The Expansive Moment: Anthropology in Britain and Africa, 1918–1970*. Cambridge: Cambridge Univ. Press.

Gouldner, Alvin. 1970. *The Coming Crisis of Western Sociology*. New York: Basic Books.

Graebner, Werner, ed. 1992. *Sokomoko: Popular Culture in East Africa*. Amsterdam: Rodopi.

Greschat, Hans-Jürgen. 1967. *Kitawala: Ursprung, Ausbreitung und Religion der Watch-Tower-Bewegung in Zentralafrika*. Marburg: N. G. Elwert.

Hannerz, Ulf. 1987. "The World in Creolization." *Africa* 57:546–59.

———. 1992. *Cultural Complexity: Studies in the Social Organization of Meaning*. New York: Columbia Univ. Press.

Hansen, Karen Tranberg. 1989. *Distant Companions: Servants and Employers in Zambia, 1900–1985*. Ithaca: Cornell Univ. Press.

Harding, Frances. 1993. "Review of J. Fabian, *Power and Performance*." *Bulletin of the School of Oriental Studies* 56 (3).

Hecht, David, and Maliqualim Simone. 1994. *Invisible Governance: The Art of African Micropolitics*. Brooklyn: Autonomedia.

Huxley, Julian. 1949. "UNESCO: Its Purpose and Its Philosophy." In *Ideological Differences and World Order*, ed. F. S. C. Northrop, 305–22. New Haven: Yale Univ. Press.

Hymes, Dell. 1974. *Foundations in Sociolinguistics: An Ethnographic Approach*. Philadelphia: Univ. of Pennsylvania Press.

Jewsiewicki, Bogumil. 1976. "La contestation sociale et la naissance du prolétariat au Zaire au cours de la première moitié du XXe siècle." *Canadian Journal of African Studies* 10:47–71.

———. 1979. "Zaire Enters the World System: Its Colonial Incorporation as the Belgian Congo." In *The Political Economy of Underdevelopment*, ed. Guy Gran, 29–53. New York: Praeger.

———. 1986. "Collective Memory and the Stakes of Power: A Reading of Popular Zairean Discourses." *History in Africa* 13:195–223.

———. 1988. "Mémoire collective et passé présent dans les discours historiques populaires zairois." In *Dialoguer avec le léopard? Pratiques, savoirs et actes du peuple face au politique en Afrique noire contemporaine,* ed. Bogumil Jewsiewicki and Henri Moniot, 218–68. Paris: Harmattan.

———. 1991. "Painting in Zaire: From the Invention of the West to Representation of Social Self." In *Africa Explores: Twentieth Century African Art,* ed. Susan Vogel and Ima Ebong, 130–51. New York: Center for African Art.

———, ed. 1992. *Art pictural zaïrois.* Sillery PQ: Editions du Septentrion.

———, ed. 1993. *Naître et mourir au Zaïre: Un demi-siècle d'histoire du quotidien.* Paris: Karthala.

———. 1995. *Chéri Samba: The Hybridity of Art.* Westmount PQ: Galerie Amrad African Art.

Jewsiewicki, Bogumil, and Henri Moniot, eds. 1988. *Dialoguer avec le léopard? Pratiques, savoirs et actes du peuple face au politique en Afrique noire contemporaine.* Paris: Harmattan.

Johnson, Paul. 1993. "Colonialism's Back—and Not a Moment Too Soon. Let's Face It: Some Countries Are Just Not Fit to Govern Themselves." *New York Times Magazine,* 18 April.

Joseph, John E., and Talbot J. Taylor, eds. 1990. *Ideologies of Language.* London: Routledge.

Jules-Rosette, Bennetta. 1975. *African Apostles: Ritual and Conversion in the Church of John Maranke.* Ithaca: Cornell Univ. Press.

Kabongo-Mbaya, Philippe B. 1994. "Les églises et la lutte pour la démocratie au Zaïre." In *Belgique/Zaïre: Une histoire en quête d'avenir,* ed. Gauthier de Villers, 157–83. Brussels: CEDAF; Paris: Harmattan.

Kazadi, Pierre Cary [Kazadi wa Mukuna]. 1979. "The Origin of Zairean Modern Music: A Socio-economic Aspect." *African Urban Studies* 6: 31–39.

Keersenboom, Saskia. 1995. *Word, Sound, Image: The Life of the Tamil Text.* Oxford: Berg.

Keil, Charles. 1987. "Participatory Discrepancies and the Power of Music." *Cultural Anthropology* 2:275–83.

Klei, Jos van der, ed. 1995. *Popular Culture: Africa, Asia and Europe.* CERES/CNWS Proceedings Summer School 1994. Utrecht: CERES.

Kramer, Fritz. 1993. *The Red Fez: Art and Spirit Possession in Africa.* London: Verso.

Lanternari, Vittorio. 1963. *The Religions of the Oppressed: A Study of Modern Messianic Cults*. New York: Mentor.

Lavie, Smadar, Kirin Narayan, and Renato Rosaldo, eds. 1993. *Creativity/Anthropology*. Ithaca: Cornell Univ. Press.

Leclerc, Gérard. 1971. *Anthropologie et colonialisme: Essai sur l'histoire de l'africanisme*. Paris: Fayard.

Leyder, Jean. 1947. "Le graphisme et l'expression graphique au Congo Belge." *Vétérans Coloniaux*, no. 5:3–5.

Lipsitz, George. 1990. *Time Passages: Collective Memory and American Popular Culture*. Minneapolis: Univ. of Minnesota Press.

Löfgren, Orval. 1989. "The Nationalization of Culture." *Ethnologia Europaea* 19:5–24.

Low, John. 1982. *Shaba Diary: A Trip to Rediscover the "Katanga" Guitar Styles and Songs of the 1950's and '60's*. Acta Ethnologica et Linguistica 54. Wien-Föhrenau: Elisabeth Stiglmayr.

Macquet-Tombu, Jeanne. 1947. "La protection des arts et métiers indigènes du Congo Belge." *Vétérans Coloniaux*, no. 7:3–12.

Marcoux, Marcene. 1982. *Cursillo: Anatomy of a Movement*. New York: Lambeth Press.

Marcus, Greil. 1989. *Lipstick Traces: A Secret History of the Twentieth Century*. Cambridge: Harvard Univ. Press.

Martin, Marie-Louise. 1975. *Kimbangu: An African Prophet and His Church*. Oxford: Basil Blackwell.

Martin, Phyllis M. 1995. *Leisure and Society in Colonial Brazzaville*. Cambridge: Cambridge Univ. Press.

Masolo, D. A. 1994. *African Philosophy in Search of Identity*. Bloomington: Indiana Univ. Press.

Matongo, Albert B. K. 1992. "Popular Culture in a Colonial Society: Another Look at Mbeni and Kalela Dances on the Copperbelt, 1930–64." In *Guardians of Their Time: Experiences of Zambians under Colonial Rule, 1890–1964*, ed. Samuel N. Chipungu, 180–217. London: Macmillan.

Mbiti, John S. 1990. *African Religions and Philosophy*. 1969. 2d ed. Portsmouth NH: Heinemann.

Milingo, Emmanuel. 1984. *The World in Between: Christian Healing and the Struggle for Spiritual Survival*. London: C. Hurst.

Miller, Daniel. 1987. *Material Culture and Mass Consumption*. Oxford: Basil Blackwell.

Mitchell, J. C. 1956. *The Kalela Dance.* Rhodes Livingstone Paper 27. Manchester: Manchester Univ. Press.
Mortier, Florent. 1947. "Enquête relative à la recherche et l'étude de dessins de jeunes primitifs du Congo belge." *Vétérans Coloniaux,* no. 4:3–9.
Mudimbe, V. Y. 1988. *The Invention of Africa: Gnosis, Philosophy, and the Order of Knowledge.* Bloomington: Indiana Univ. Press.
———, ed. 1992. *The Surreptitious Speech: Présence Africaine and the Politics of Otherness, 1974–1987.* Chicago: Univ. of Chicago Press.
Mukerji, Chandra, and Michael Schudson, eds. 1991. *Rethinking Popular Culture: Contemporary Perspectives in Cultural Studies.* Berkeley: Univ. of California Press.
Munn, Nancy D. 1992. "The Cultural Anthropology of Time: A Critical Essay." *Annual Review of Anthropology* 21:93–123.
Mwene-Batende. 1982. *Mouvements messianiques et protestation sociale: Le cas du Kitawala chez les Kumu du Zaïre.* Kinshasa: Faculté de Théologie Catholique.
Nederveen-Pieterse, Jan. 1992. *White on Black: Images of Africa and Blacks in Western Popular Culture.* New Haven: Yale Univ. Press.
Newbury, Catharine. 1994. "Introduction: Paradoxes of Democratization in Africa." *African Studies Review* 37 (1): 1–8.
Ngũgĩ wa Thiong'o. 1993. *Moving the Centre: The Struggle for Cultural Freedoms.* London: James Currey.
Noyes, John K. 1992. *Colonial Space: Spatiality in the Discourse of German South West Africa, 1884–1915.* Chur, Switzerland: Harwood Academic.
Obiechina, E. 1973. *An African Popular Literature: A Study of Onitsha Market Pamphlets.* Cambridge: Cambridge Univ. Press.
Omasombo, Jean Tshonda, ed. 1993. *Le Zaïre à l'épreuve de l'histoire immédiate: Hommage à Benoît Verhaegen.* Paris: Karthala.
Ortner, Sherry B. 1984. "Theory in Anthropology since the Sixties." *Comparative Studies in Society and History* 4:121–42.
———. 1995. "Resistance and the Problem of Ethnographic Refusal." *Comparative Studies in Society and History* 37:173–93.
Parkin, David. 1993. "Nemi in the Modern World: Return of the Exotic." *Man* 28:79–99.
Peacock, James L. 1968. *Rites of Modernization: Symbolic and Social Aspects of Indonesian Proletarian Theater.* Chicago: Univ. of Chicago Press.

Périer, Gaston-Denys. 1947. "Regards sur l'art graphique indigène au Congo Belge." *Vétérans Coloniaux,* no. 8:3–14.

———. 1948. *Les arts populaires du Congo Belge.* Brussels: Office de Publicité.

Périer, Gaston-Denys, and Jean Leyder. 1947–48. "Essai de bibliographie chronologique sur le graphisme et l'expression graphique au Congo Belge et dans les régions avoisinantes (1974–1900)." *Vétérans Coloniaux,* no. 12:3–7; *Revue Coloniale Illustrée* 20 (1): 43–48, 20 (2): 39–47.

Poewe, Karla, ed. 1994. *Charismatic Christianity as Global Culture.* Columbia: Univ. of South Carolina Press.

Poujol, G., and R. Labourie, eds. 1979. *Les cultures populaires.* Toulouse: Privat.

Powdermaker, Hortense. 1962. *Copper Town: Changing Africa. The Human Situation on the Rhodesian Copperbelt.* New York: Harper & Row.

Ranger, Terence O. 1975. *Dance and Society in Eastern Africa.* Berkeley: Univ. of California Press.

Riegl, Alois. 1978. *Volkskunst, Hausfleiss und Hausindustrie.* 1893. Mittenwald, Germany: Mäander.

Roberts, Allen F. 1984. "'Fishers of Men': Religion and Political Economy among the Colonized Tabwa." *Africa* 54 (2): 49–70.

Rooij, Vincent A., de. 1996. *Cohesion through Contrast: Discourse Structure in Shaba Swahili/French Conversations.* Amsterdam: IFOTT.

Rowe, William, and Vivian Schelling. 1991. *Memory and Modernity: Popular Culture in Latin America.* London: Verso.

Said, Edward W. 1993. *Culture and Imperialism.* London: Vintage.

Schatzberg, Michael G. 1988. *The Dialectics of Oppression in Zaire.* Bloomington: Indiana Univ. Press.

———. 1993. "Power, Legitimacy, and 'Democratization' in Africa." *Africa* 63:445–61.

Scott, James C. 1985. *Weapons of the Weak: Everyday Forms of Peasant Resistance.* New Haven: Yale Univ. Press.

Shiach, Morag. 1989. *Discourse on Popular Culture: Class, Gender and History in Cultural Analysis, 1730 to the Present.* Stanford: Stanford Univ. Press.

Siegel, James T. 1986. *Solo in the New Order: Language and Hierarchy in an Indonesian City.* Princeton: Princeton Univ. Press.

Smet, A. J., ed. 1975. *Philosophie africaine: Textes choisis et bibliographie selective.* 2 vols. Kinshasa: Presses Universitaires du Zaire.

Stocking, George W., Jr. 1968. *Race, Culture, and Evolution: Essays in the History of Anthropology*. New York: Free Press.

Stolcke, Verena. 1995. "Talking Culture: New Boundaries, New Rhetorics of Exclusion in Europe." *Current Anthropology* 36:1–24.

Szombati-Fabian, Ilona, and Johannes Fabian. 1976. "Art, History and Society: Popular Painting in Shaba, Zaire." *Studies in the Anthropology of Visual Communication* 3:1–21.

Taussig, Michael. 1993. *Mimesis and Alterity: A Particular History of the Senses*. New York: Routledge.

Tempels, Placide. [1948]. *Catéchèse bantoue*. Bruges: Abbaye de St. André.

———. 1959. *Bantu Philosophy*. Paris: Présence Africaine.

Ter Haar, Gerrie. 1992. *Spirit of Africa: The Healing Ministry of Archbishop Milingo in Zambia*. Trenton NJ: Africa World Press.

Thompson Drewal, Margaret. 1991. "The State of Research on Performance in Africa." *African Studies Review* 34 (3): 1–64.

Tonkin, Elizabeth. 1992. *Narrating Our Pasts: The Social Construction of Oral History*. Cambridge: Cambridge Univ. Press.

Turner, Thomas Edwin. 1993. "'Batetela,' 'Baluba,' 'Basonge': Ethnogenesis in Zaire." *Cahiers d'Etudes Africaines* 33:587–612.

Van Binsbergen, Wim. 1995. "Popular Culture: The Dynamics of African Cultural and Ethnic Identity in a Context of Globalization." In *Popular Culture: Africa, Asia, and Europe*, ed. J. van der Klei, 7–40. Proceedings Summer School CERES/CNWS 1994. Utrecht: CERES/CNWS.

Vansina, Jan. 1961. *De la tradition orale: Essai de méthode historique*. Tervuren, Belgium: Musée Royal de l'Afrique Centrale.

———. 1985. *Oral Tradition as History*. Madison: Univ. of Wisconsin Press.

———. 1986. "Afterthoughts on the Historiography of Oral Tradition." In *African Historiographies: What History for Which Africa?* ed. Bogumil Jewsiewicki and David Newbury, 105–10. Beverly Hills CA: Sage.

———. 1994. *Living with Africa*. Madison: Univ. of Wisconsin Press.

Vellut, Jan-Luc. 1987. "Résistance et espaces de liberté dans l'histoire coloniale du Zaire: Avant la marche à l'indépendance, ca. 1876–1945." In *Rébellions-révolutions au Zaire, 1963–1965*, ed. C. Coquery-Vidrovitch, A. Forest, and H. Weiss, 1:24–73. Paris: Harmattan.

Verhaegen, Benoît. 1974. *Introduction à l'histoire immédiate: Essai de méthodologie qualitative*. Gembloux, Belgium: Duculot.

Wagner, Roy. 1975. *The Invention of Culture*. Englewood Cliffs NJ: Prentice-Hall.

White, Hayden. 1980. "The Value of Narrativity in the Representation of Reality." *Critical Inquiry* 7:5–27.

White, Louise. 1990. *The Comforts of Home: Prostitution in Colonial Nairobi*. Chicago: Univ. of Chicago Press.

Index

Italicized page numbers refer to illustrations.